DA ALT GESHIKHTEM

(THE OLD STORIES)

DAVID SELCER

In Memory of Lester Selcer

ISBN: 978-1-62249-479-8

Published by
Biblio Publishing
Columbus, Ohio
BiblioPublishng.com

Table of Contents

Preface

Forced migrations are a salient feature of the present century, as they were in the last century. Only the reasons, the countries of origin, and the countries where sanctuary is sought are different. Treatment of downtrodden immigrants when forced to migrate has been the same for over 125 years for the most part. Blocked passage, refusal of entry, the separation of children from parents, legal barriers, low paying jobs, or interment in displaced persons camps have occurred everywhere, including the United States, regardless of who the immigrants are or where they come from.

In the first third of the 20th Century millions of Jews entered the United States from Russia fleeing pogroms and other injustices, Chinese people and other East Asians entered as laborers, and millions of Italians and Slavs entered from central and southeastern Europe looking for better lives. In the middle of the 20th Century thousands of Jews fled Europe for Palestine before Israel came into being. Now, in the first third of the Twenty-First Century, hundreds of thousands of Mexicans, and Central Americans have crossed the borders illegally into the United States.

The Old Stories is about an immigrant and about forced immigration. It falls into the category of historical fiction. Yet all its main characters lived, in fact, under the same names they carry in the book, although some were later anglicized at the hands of immigration officers and others. The circumstances and surroundings the book's characters find themselves in really happened, and they are all historically correct, although experienced in many cases by people other than the book's characters.

The protagonist of *The Old Stories*, Chaim Zelitzer ha'Levi, a/k/a Hyman Zeltzer, comes to Canada from the Ukraine during the Russo-Japanese War of 1904-05, via an unconventional route--through Siberia and across the Pacific Ocean. He has deserted the Russian Navy at Vladivostok during the first great wave of immigration out of the Russian Empire before Soviet Communism.

When he finally reaches the United states, he chooses to aid Jews participating in the last years of the second and greatest wave of immigration to Palestine, known as "Aliyah Bet." They are from Eastern Europe (Poland, Lithuania, Latvia, Hungary, Rumania and Russia). World War Two has just ended and the people Zeltzer is saving are from the concentration camps.

"Palestine" in this book means the part of British Mandatory Palestine that became the State of Israel on May 15, 1948. "Palestinian" means a Jew who lived in that area.

"Aliyah Bet" was a clandestine movement that brought Jews from Europe to Palestine by sea from 1934 to 1948. The British called it illegal immigration and tried to prevent it. During the three year period from the defeat of the Nazis in 1945 and the establishment of the State of Israel in May 1948, North American Jews, with the help of the Haganah which was the Jewish underground organization, purchased war surplus Coast Guard and other ships, as well as out-dated commercial vessels to transport holocaust survivors to Palestine. There were twelve of these ships, and they were all purchased secretly and manned almost completely by North American Jews with Palestinian officers.

The Tradewinds, later named the Hatikvah, was one of these vessels. In *The Old Stories*, Hyman Zeltzer sails on this vessel. It was an actual ship, a Coast Guard cutter, which embarked passengers on two successive nights at beaches in Italy, that was captured at sea and taken to Haifa on May 17, 1947. It carried 1,414 Jewish immigrants, plus crew members, all of whom were interned in Cyprus DP (displaced persons) camps.

The actual North American members of Hatikvah's crew were: Hy Braverman, Hal Galili (Fineberg), Sam Gordon, Murray S. Greenfield, Harold Katz, Paul Kaye (Kaminetzky), Bernie Levy, Josh Lewis, Hugh McDonald, Al Nemoff, Mike Perlstein, Adrian Phillips, Arnie Reuben, Gerald Rubestein, P. Rubin, Leo Slefstein, Manny (Wingy) Weinseine, Marvin Weiss and Saul Yellin.

The actual names of certain people appearing in this book are as follows:

Captain William C. Ash, an American professional mariner, born in Poland, who served as a key "Aliyah Bet" volunteer, instrumental in buying and equipping "Aliyah Bet" vessels in the United States, and in recruiting and training their crews:

Ernest Bevin, the British Foreign Secretary who was a vocal opponent of "Aliyah Bet" and Jewish immigration to Palestine; and,

Ze'ev (Danny) Schind, the Palestinian director of "Aliyah Bet" activities in the United States who went to New York in 1946 and organized the buying and equipping of vessels and recruiting of crews.

Many of the historical facts contained in *The Old Stories* may be found in Hochstein, Jos. M. and Greenfield, Murray S., *The Jews' Secret Fleet.* Gefen Publishing House, Jerusalem & New York, 1987: especially those concerning the raising of the fleet; the sailing of the Hatikvah, and the battle of the Hatikvah, its crew and passengers against British destroyers. Other sources were Stone, I.F., *Underground to Palestine.* Boni & Gaer, New York, 1946, especially his descriptions of the passengers of the Wedgewood and Haganah, which were the first American manned ships; and, Orbach, Michael, *The Hatikvah sailed on: Paul Kaye hero of Aliyah Bet tells his story*, The Jewish

David Selcer

Star, New York, April 2010, a journalists interview concerning the feelings of a Hatikvah crew member upon first seeing Holocaust survivors boarding his ship, and upon the blowing up of the British prison transport ship Empire Lifeguard.

Yiddish, Hebrew and Russian terms used but not explained in this book are:

bissel --Yiddish for little

bulvan--Yiddish for bull

bris or brit--Hebrew for circumcision and sign of covenant with God

chassid--Yiddish for ultra-orthodox Jew; also means happy one

cheder--Hebrew for class or Hebrew school

chutzpah--Yiddish for outrageous nerve

gonif--Yiddish for thief

goyim--Yiddish for the "other" or non-Jews

idti izdes--Russian for come here

mitzvah--Yiddish for good deed

kugel--Yiddish for Jewish noodle dish

kvas--Russian for drink of fermented wheat flavored with raisins

moreh--Hebrew for teacher

mensch--Yiddish for gentleman or human being

schul--Yiddish for synagogue

shidkh--Yiddish for matchmaker

shiddokh--Yiddish for the match

rogelachen--Yiddish for small rolled fruit or cheese cakes.

traifeneh smutz--Yiddish for prohibited dirt

yarmelka--Yiddish for skullcap

Zohar, Mishnah & Tenach—All Jewish holy books written in Hebrew, the latter being the Jewish Bible

Prologue

"The worm in the radish doesn't think there is anything sweeter."

—**Sholem Aleichem**

At a table in a classroom sits a disheveled boy bending over a book, leaning on his elbows beneath sunken shoulders, his skinny chest heaving rhythmically, his *yarmulke* askew. It's yet another boring day in the *cheder*. Again his eyes have glazed over, fighting off sleep, as he attempts to attack the Hebrew letters spread before him on the page, like old bones. The dream that comes is always the same.

After all, how much is there to dream about in Russia at the end of the Nineteenth Century when you're nine years old? A river bank dotted with pear trees. Rowboats plying the waters of the Ingulets River near its junction with the Dnieper. A rare family picnic on the grassy shore, away from the city with all its noise, its smoke and the clanking of horse-carts in the streets all day long. He dreams of bread and jam with butter, herring and smoked fish with horse radish, cucumbers, pies, kugel and watermelon, spread across a tablecloth on dark green grass, and plenty of kvas to drink. His seven sisters are running gaily along the river's edge, and there are no young scholars with halitosis sitting around spouting interpretations of the Talmud, and making him look stupid from his lack of knowledge; no "intellectuals" ignoring him, who do not know him, and are not like him. They are all back at the *cheder,* engrossed in study.

1

David Selcer

At 17, Chaim ben Eliezer HaLevi, otherwise known as
Chaim Zelitzer, would cross the Pacific Ocean on his own to
live in North America and have his name changed to Hyman
Zeltzer. The young scholars, on the other hand would perish
for the most part. And at 55, he would cross the Atlantic
Ocean with volunteers, many of whom were half his age, to
rescue their remnant. But on that day in class, he was just a
gangly nine-year-old boy, bored by his study of the ancient
prophets and tired from his early morning's work in his
uncle's metal shop before dawn.

Warmth from the sun streams down on him through the
stained glass window above in the Great Choral Synagogue
of Kherson, as his face is about to drop into the spine of his
book. "Chaim," yells the *moreh,* twisting him by the ear!
"Again? Again you're sleeping? You're the worst student
in the class. How can you ever have any hope to emulate a
righteous person if you don't even know what a righteous
person is. To learn what is a righteous person, you must
study, not sleep."

Chaim hated to study, not to read, but to study. His
favorite books were Sholem Aleichem's stories about the
Jewish Holidays, not the boring tales of the prophets in the
Tenakh and the *Mishnah.* Yet he did aspire to becoming a
righteous person, or a *Tzadik* as they were sometimes called.
His understanding of that phrase was that a righteous person
was one who did the right thing, who followed the laws in
the Torah, who gave to charity and who was just in his ways
toward others, to the point where his merit surpassed his
iniquity. Unfortunately, his teachers and the other students
in his class held a divergent, more complicated, more studied
metaphysical view.

To them, a Tzadik is one who has
completely sublimated his natural "animal" or "vital" soul
inclinations into holiness, so that he experiences only love
and awe of God, without material temptations. A Tzadik
serves as a "vehicle" to God and has no ego or self-

2

consciousness. A person cannot attain such a level. Rather it is granted from on High, and to be emulated, although one will fail inevitably from time to time. This, they have gleaned from hours of comparing Maimonides' definition of a Tzadik, based on the Babylonian Talmud, to those of the Hasidic rabbis and the Kabbalah, based on the Zohar and the Jerusalem Talmud, and then memorizing it all.

Chaim didn't care about the derision heaped on him by his teacher. Because at home he received the acceptance of his father and his uncle for being a skilled apprentice metal worker who, at a younger age than most, was given great responsibility. He liked learning a practical skill. In the world outside the *cheder,* he liked dealing with adults and pleasing customers. He like being treated as a man, while others his age spent time at the *cheder* learning otherworldly and spiritual things by rote instead of doing real work.

By thirteen he barely made it through his *bar mitzvah,* as his parents sat in the synagogue praying for his success in the chanting his *Torah* portion. Afterwards, he learned that the adulation of the Jewish community was turning away from him and toward his fellow students. They were either going on to the *Yeshiva* to become rabbis, soforim, and cantors, or becoming members of the Enlightenment or, *haskalah,* which was the Jewish intellectual movement of Central and Eastern Europe leading to the secularization of Judaism, more cultural assimilation and to Zionism. Either path left Chaim out, which confused, even saddened him.

To make things worse, his older brother, his only brother, had received one of those gifts from on High, as if it were that which Chaim's fellow *cheder* students espoused as needed to make a *Tzadik.* His brother Shmuel had received a beautiful god given voice, and it was quickly making him one of the most famous cantors in the Ukrainian province of Russia, as well as the pride of his family. Shmuel was a true spiritual leader. And Chaim was supposed to be happy about it.

David Selcer

"Don't worry his father told him. You will earn your accomplishments in life, not receive them as a gifts from on High. They will come from inside you. And I will get you to America, one way or another, where they will be appreciated. I promise this to you. And you will make everyone around you proud."

ONE

"No matter how bad things get, you got to go on living, even if it kills you."

-- Sholem Aleichem

January 1974

At 87, Hyman Zeltzer was a robust, barrel-chested man with a wispy shock of white hair flapping across his bald head in the breeze – a big bear of a Russian. He had a kind, infectious uncontrollable laugh – almost always too loud, but lately, more often than not, deteriorating into a dry coughing spell. A simple man, he mostly did what he was told, having learned early in life that following his personal urges too often brought danger to him, whereas following the rules and showing respect like a hat-in-hand peasant were the safest ways to go.

At least, as his son, that's the way I saw him. What others saw was apparently different.

He was as loyal to his wife as a German Shepherd is to its master, always doing what she wanted, when she wanted, and how she wanted it done. He took all his cues for living life the American way from her. It was his wife, Anne, who made a family for him in the United States. It was she who helped him with his English and helped him set up a business so he would not have to labor for a living solely with his hands. It was she who brought him to Cleveland, Ohio where he thrived. She was also the impetus for his moving to Miami to retire, and then moving back to Cleveland to be with extended family

5

She was the brains of the family and he was the brawn. This he knew. As in so many other migrant Jewish homes of the time, as I saw things, Ma ran Pa's life.

According to the eulogy the Rabbi gave for him at his funeral, there was another Hyman Zeltzer, one that few knew, one that grew to adulthood in the latter days of the Russian Empire, a Hyman Zeltzer I never saw or met, with half his heart in the old traditions of his youth, and the other half aspiring toward the new ways of the 20th Century.

The other Hyman Zeltzer never hesitated to defend himself, his family or his friends. When the defense of his family or a friend was at stake, he let nothing stop him – not finances, not the everyday conventions of the moment, not rules, regulations, traditions or the law, not even soldiers or the police. He also would try anything once, no matter how daunting the task. "It wasn't *chutzpah* on his part," said the Rabbi. "It was bravery."

He was carelessly, almost recklessly, brave and would stubbornly follow his own heedless ideas concerning the protection of his family and others, no matter the consequences to his own well-being. When uncontrolled, he might act rashly, making spur of the moment decisions to help those in need without regard to the greater consequences or circumstances at large.

As an example, my father borrowed money with no means to repay it in order to get my brother, Ben, a violin and send him to music school. He could have rented the instrument more cheaply and waited to see if Ben showed a proclivity toward music. Some might have thought this very sacrificing or loving on his part; others, that it was foolish or stupid.

"Many took his disregard of the subtler aspects of dangerous situations for courage," said the Rabbi. *Or, was it that he simply had no appreciation for the jeopardy into which he was placing himself,* I wondered. He was confusing, so confusing that I often took him to be acting out of a lack of intelligence. For instance, after he and his wife retired to Miami where his seven-year-old grandson (my son) visited them, a large scorpion waddled out from under the bed, scaring the boy. Dad stomped on it bare foot, heedless of the insect's ability to poison.

On the other hand, one could say he often stubbornly placed the needs of others ahead of his own to the point where even good logic wouldn't stop him once he'd made up his mind to help another person. For instance, though he'd grown to love Florida after retiring there, when my brother Ben, who lived in Cleveland, began getting sick from a chronic debilitating illness in 1961, my father gave up Florida, sold his house, went back to work, and returned to Cleveland where his wife and he could be of help to Ben and his family. But Pa was by no means a rich enough man just to give up his home in Florida and do this.

Now I ask you, in all good conscience. What would you have done in that situation if you were a 74-year-old man? Well, Pa would listen to no argument against moving back, no argument about finances. No argument about his own needs. And no argument about how much he loved Florida. Often in similar situations where intellect, exigency or education might have given others pause, his stubborn single mindedness kept him moving toward his decisions.

By the time he turned 87, as I saw it, nothing had changed his bullheadedness, or as others saw it, his heedlessness of his own needs. Then came his final sacrifice for another person.

Thirteen years after returning to Cleveland, fate separated him from his wife when she was admitted to The Cleveland Clinic with painful kidney stones. At the same time, he languished at University Hospitals with an oversized bleeding prostate. But he simply wasn't about to let their health conditions separate them. Who knew what they could be doing to his wife over there at that "other" hospital. And he wouldn't be there to stop them. Nobody would.

Removing his IV and disconnecting his heart monitor, he got out of his hospital bed, dressed and exited University Hospitals in a driving rain, taking the Euclid Avenue bus a few miles west toward the Cleveland Clinic. There, he checked himself in and asked to be placed in the same room with his wife, where he knew he could watch over her.

"Mr. Zeltzer! Mr. Zeltzer!" the University Hospitals nurses yelled after him. "You can't do this! Where are you going?"

All, to no avail. I thought his actions on this occasion were positively stupid. But Pa always had his reasons. Not always right, but never in doubt. That was Pa.

University Hospitals' Law Department called me at home, as his health custodian with power of attorney, shortly after he left. "It's all about the liability," the hospital's representative insisted. "University Hospitals can no longer be responsible for Hyman Zeltzer's well-being." And the representative was right.

Pa's wife's kidney stones passed. But three-and-a-half weeks later, Hyman Zeltzer was dead of bilateral pneumococcal pneumonia. Until then, nobody, except his wife, even knew the year he was born. Indeed, for sixty-seven years, nobody except his wife, bothered to remember his birthday when it rolled around.

At his funeral his year of birth was indicated as 1889, but nobody knew the exact date because when he was born, Russia was still using the Julian calendar, not the Gregorian calendar, and the Julian calendar was approximately thirteen days behind the Gregorian calendar, depending on the year. Nor did most people know where he was born. I always thought it was Russia, but it wasn't.

It was Kherson Oblast in the Ukraine, not far from Odessa, a fact that came out in his eulogy. I didn't know his father's name was Eliezer Ha Levi or that his mother's name was Deborah. In truth, I knew very little about my father, because frankly, as a first generation American, I was more interested in hiding him from everyone in my life than finding out anything about him. I wanted to go to college, to become a business man; or maybe even a professional, an accountant. I wanted to speak English and to be spoken to in English, not Russian, not Yiddish and not Hebrew. I wanted a life of Horatio Alger for myself, not the life of the son of an immigrant Jew.

So I didn't know that my father was born at home in Kherson during the reign of Czar Alexander III, or that on the day he was born, that city of about 90,000 inhabitants, was graced with another *pogrom*. Outside the house of his birth, the Cossacks were tearing up floorboards from Jewish porches, chasing after women and destroying livestock. Somebody had murdered Czar Alexander II recently, and the Jews were going to pay for it. It wasn't the first *pogrom*, in that part of the Ukraine, and it wouldn't be the last. A myriad of things constantly triggered Jew hate.

TWO

"When you die, others who think they know you, will concoct things about you... Better pick up a pen and write it yourself, for you know yourself best."
Sholem Aleichem

My father didn't have a birth certificate because of the pogrom going on at his birth. Things were very bad then— so bad that his family had to hold his *Bris* secretly. God forbid the Cossacks should find out a Jewish boy was being circumcised in the neighborhood! Circumcision, the sign of the covenant Jews supposedly had with God, was a symbol in the minds of gentiles of the Jews' supposed "chosen people" status, and it enraged the Russian Orthodox priests, who labelled it a pagan blood ritual.

The thought that somehow "the chosen people," had their own *brit* with God, was also enough to infuriate the Cossacks and others too. Others who sanctimoniously went about proclaiming that anyone who failed to accept Christ as God could not go to Heaven. If the Cossacks discovered a Bris going on, it would trigger certain hell for everyone attending, not symbolic hell, but the actual demonstrative destruction of their property and their peace of mind—in short, a palpable demonstration of Russian anti-Semitism in the old fashioned way. So Hyman's father just forgot about getting him a birth certificate because of all the turmoil of the pogrom occurring at the time of his birth. At his Bris, Hyman was named Chaim ben Eliezer Ha Levi, and everyone felt that was good enough for the family, the community, and for God. The addition of a Russian birth certificate was superfluous.

Hyman Zeltzer died leaving behind my very sick mother, my brother, Ben, myself, and our families. It was only then that I began finding out who and what he really was. Indeed, there was a third Hyman Zeltzer of whom only I alone would come to know, and only posthumously.

On the day of his funeral, the previously unknown details of his life began seeping out in the eulogy that was delivered for him. Ma must have spent hours with the rabbi meticulously filling him in on these things. *Apparently she actually loved Hyman,* which was something I really never bothered to think about before. A mother and a father are just there, as far as a child is concerned, like a house, a school or a car. That there should be any love between them, let alone romantic love, is inconceivable. They are just *there,* like the front door, the windows in the house and the front lawn. Appreciation for what they really were, or for what they had together, doesn't come until many years later, if at all.

My father's funeral was totally enervating to me. It literally weakened my knees and made me just want to go to bed. The Cantor chanted the Hebrew prayer—"*Ale Moleh Rachamim*"—something about Hyman Zeltzer's soul finding solace under the wings of God. It didn't make any sense to me, not even symbolic sense. After the funeral, sitting at the dining room table in Ma's house in University Heights with all the mirrors covered, I mindlessly watched people slowly mounting the steps to the porch, washing their hands in silver bowels and using the white towels provided at the open front door to dry their hands. They were rinsing Pa's death away, so they could come in and pay their respects. Symbolism! Why were they washing their hands? What good would that do?

My brother, our wives, Ma and my children were all there, sitting on the low stools that had been provided for the mourners. Why *low* stools? Tradition! But I preferred to sit

11

at the table, separated from the remnants of my family's long gone orthodox Jewish tradition, and tortured with after-the-fact thoughts. *How could I not have known anything about my father before? Why did the hearse not take his remains to the Beth Emet cemetery for interment in Cleveland?* Instead, his body was whisked away to the airport, and from there, flown to Israel for burial in some cemetery on some kibbutz of which I'd never heard. *Why,* I wondered? That in itself was solid evidence that I knew very little about my father.

"Don't play with it, Jody," I told my brother's daughter, who was monkeying with the tall red memorial candle atop the fire-place mantel. "You'll start a fire." She was trying to blow it out. Hmh—*wonder if that would bring some sort of curse or something down on us,* I thought to myself? *Paganism! That's a very paganist way of thinking. More importantly, why did it always have to fall to me to discipline my brother's kids?* The answer to that was more understandable. It was because Ben and his wife were sensitive people—too sensitive, too liberal too easy-going and free with their children about everything. They were artists! Bohemians! I felt it was somehow my duty to teach their kids how to live in the real world, like regular human beings.

When will the women serve us, I keep thinking? We Jews sit *shiva,* (our wake) after a funeral, and the custom is for everyone to come into the house and mill around while the immediate family sits and eats. *Why?* Nobody else eats anything until the family has finished eating. The food is always served by women in the kitchen who are friends of the family, not relatives, but friends. *Why?* Frankly, I prefer Irish wakes. They're much more fun, and they accomplish the same thing—closure!

Finally! The rabbi arrives and gives the blessing over the bread. As we eat, my mind keeps wandering back to the eulogy he'd delivered. "Chaim was the eighth child in a family of nine siblings, the youngest of only two boys." It's all news to me. Nobody had ever told me about his family.

"He never learned to read any letters but Hebrew letters, which were the alphabetic characters in which the language of Yiddish is written. He understood Hebrew, but with these letters, he could read Yiddish well. Yiddish, in his day was the language of eleven million out of the eighteen million Jews in the world. It was mostly made up of colloquial middle German words with some Hebrew terms interspersed, and it was written in Hebrew characters.

"Chaim could easily make himself understood in Russian," the eulogy went on, "although he never had any formal Russian education, and the only Russian words he could read were the necessary ones—'stop, go, bathroom, yes, no, open, closed, left, right, exit, silence.' Thus, he never read any of the great Russian literature. Tolstoy, Nabokov, Turgenev, and Chekov all escaped him. The full length and breadth of his formal education was circumscribed by what he could glean from the *cheder* at the *bies ha mikdosh.* (classroom at the temple), which was known as The Great Choral Synagogue of Kherson. There, he studied Torah. But he was not one of the top students. This, however, did not prevent him from furtively reading some of the things written by Yiddish writers of the time.

"Otherwise, as far as his education went, it consisted of his apprenticing with his Uncle Meyer as a machinist. Kherson was an important ship building town and a large port where the Dnieper River flowed into the Black Sea. It was full of iron works and machine shop owners that subcontracted with ship builders and warehousemen for repair work and other types of skilled metal working. Uncle Meyer was one of them, an iron-worker by trade.

"Thus, Chaim did not grow up in a *shtetl* (village). Rather, according to the rabbi, he was a *shtot baucher* (city boy), who went about the streets of Kherson doing machinist's work for others—welding here and there;

drilling holes for screws to fix furniture; repairing sewing machines and any other jobs he could do with the tools from his uncle's machine shop. At the shipbuilding docks where he worked with his uncle, he learned how to machine parts for steam engines, how to fashion gears and other parts necessary for screw propulsion, and how to fix boilers. For those who could not become doctors, lawyers, or professors, if you were not in a family business, apprenticing as a tailor, a butcher or bootmaker was the second line down, but learning to be a machinist, or an iron-worker, was nothing to sneeze at either.

"And, Chaim was fortunate enough to do some travelling as a boy to Odessa with his father, who sold dry-goods. Chaim thought Odessa must be the most beautiful city in the world, with its palm trees, its beaches and its French style architecture. There, his father bought shirts and socks, dresses, aprons and tablecloths which he took back to Kherson to hold for sale, but the business was not yet big enough to accommodate another family member. Chaim also travelled on occasion with his Uncle Meyer to Kiev, the capital of the Ukraine.

In 1900, Kiev was a city which was both the heart of the Russian community in the Ukraine, having spawned the Romanov dynasty, the bloodline from which all the Czars came, and the center of the Ukraine's Jewish community, where many of the great Russian rabbis studied. At the time Kiev was awash in tensions between the Russian Orthodox Church and the Jews, as well as tensions between the Russian government in St. Petersburg and the socialists of the Ukraine. Communism was budding, but these were things that flew right by Chaim without any awareness on his part. It was as if politics was not a part of his genealogical make-up, and religiously, there were no other worlds than his Jewish world. He was oblivious to the social and political machinations affecting his life.

There was, however, according to the rabbi's eulogy,

one other educational source effecting Chaim Zelitzer, if you could call it that. "His uncle Meyer was an 'activist' who freely spouted his views. Not a religious activist, not strictly secular, nor was he an atheist, a socialist, a capitalist or a communist. Meyer was also not a monarchist, a nihilist, or a democratizer. No, Meyer was something much narrower—a Zionist. He believed with all his heart that the Jewish people should have their own nation and that it should be located in Palestine. By the end of the 19th Century, Kherson was the location of one of the main branches of the Zionist Movement.

"Thus, early in his life, Chaim's ears were filled with the ideology of Zionism—national liberation, reclaiming the land from the desert and the swamps, tilling it in collective farms, reviving Hebrew as the spoken language of the Jewish people and the secularization of the *halakha* (Jewish law) by Jewish culturalism. He could not avoid hearing about Theodore Herzl, Chaim Weitzman, Eliezer Ben Yahuda and the like from Meyer, though he preferred not to listen to all this.

"But Chaim's travels with his father and uncle had another influence on him," according to the rabbi. In Kiev, Uncle Meyer introduced him to an unlikely Zionist friend of his—Sholem Aleichem.

"Nobody else knew it except his mother," the rabbi claimed, "but Chaim read Sholem Aleichem voraciously, and the author's characters reverberated inside him. Like them, there he was, on the cusp of being stuck in the old ways, but yearning for the new, though he knew not what they were. Leaving the generation of his parents, and heading out toward he knew not what.

. . .

Thinking about Pa's eulogy triggered an annoying

15

headache that was beginning to torment me. My father, reading Shalom Aleichem? The thought of it was too much for me. Aleichem was the greatest Yiddish writer ever to live. He wrote novels, plays, and short stories, all in Yiddish. The man believed that Yiddish, once spoken by almost eleven million people, should be considered another European language, and he plotted a grammar book for it. He was sometimes called the Mark Twain of the Jews.

And my simple father supposedly read him avidly. It was hard to believe that a man with whom I absolutely could not sit at a dinner table for longer than five minutes because it was so gross to watch him eat, was an avid reader of anything. He sucked his tea through a sugar cube held between his front teeth. He ate his peas with a knife. He tied his napkin around his neck like a bib. To me, he was little more than a Russian peasant, but he was a reader of Sholem Aleichem!

There was a great dichotomy between my view of Hyman Zeltzer and the view the rabbi presented in his eulogy, so great that I begin feeling I needed to go upstairs and lay down in order to escape the emotional tension with which this day was besetting me. As in many families, it is becoming apparent to me that either overly embellished truths are being told and myths are being manufactured to fit the occasion, or I really do not know my father. In any event, there is nothing I can do about it now. My forehead is throbbing.

THREE

"This is an ugly and mean world, and only to spite it we mustn't weep. If you want to know, this is the constant source of my good spirit, of my humor. Not to cry, out of spite, only to laugh out of spite, only to laugh."

Sholem Aleichem

I sleep as soon as my head hits the pillow; then awaken; and then sleep again. Dreams drift into my slowly disappearing consciousness, invading my subconscious, carrying me back to Kherson, although I'd never been there. Pa had no birth certificate I keep remembering as I fall in and out of nap mode. Finally, I succumb to sound sleep.

It's 1903, and I'm riding behind Pa and his Uncle Meyer in a four-wheeled wagon with rubber tires, drawn by Kasha and another horse named Victor. Pa looks very big for his age. In my dream, I keep seeing Kasha's head and neck rhythmically bobbing between the hames on his horseshoe collar, up and down, as the soft-tired wagon quietly passes down Nekravsova Street toward the Suverovskyi District.

My sub-conscious has confused this wagon with a junk wagon I'd seen later as a young boy in Cleveland that had soft air-filled pneumatic tires. When Pa was a boy, they didn't have rubber tires that were filled with air. The finest of carriages had only hard rubber rimmed wheels.

The day is chilly, as we pass colored stucco houses, pink, yellow and white, with red tile roofs, and then a stodgy looking stone building, which must be a cathedral, judging from its pillared stone portico and golden dome. It's late in the Spring, and the Cottonwood trees are filling the steel

17

grey sky with floating seeds like a light snow. Today is different from other days because the wagon is not filled with Meyer's tools and machines headed for the ship-building docks to mill parts on contract for vessels being built by the ship builders. Instead, five goats occupy the back of his vehicle, headed to the central market for sale and slaughter. Pa has raised them inside the tottering fence surrounding the heavily weeded unkempt backyard behind the Zelitzer's unpainted wooden frame house.

"So, Chaim," Meyer says, turning to Pa, and putting on a teasing air. "What can I tell you about yourself today? Huh? What do you want to learn?"

"I don't know uncle. Tell me what you think I should know."

It's amazing, because their conversation is in Yiddish, a language of which I have no command. Yet I understand every word they are saying. True, it's impossible to grow up in an immigrant Jewish household like mine without picking up a few Yiddish words here and there, but it's not true that I can either speak or understand the language. I know only a *bissel.* It is the language my father and my mother use when they don't want me to know what they're saying, a foreign silly sounding language to me. But in my dream I am understanding it.

Challenged by Chaim's question, Meyer says, "Well, for instance, did you know you're a 'momzer?'"

Wait a minute! A momzer is a bastard. What kind of thing is this for an uncle to call his nephew?

Chaim protests vehemently. "I'm no momzer. If I were, I'd probably be living in the children's home waiting for somebody to come and adopt me. Instead, I live at home with my brother and sisters, and with my parents. So how can I be a momzer?" I could not imagine how uncomfortable Uncle Meyer's comment must be making Chaim—to be called a bastard by his own uncle, an assertion that placed in doubt the very fact that Meyer was indeed his

18

true uncle.

"You have no birth certificate," Meyer replies calmly, reveling in the fact that his teasing had gotten under the fourteen-year-old's skin. "Without a birth certificate, you're a momzer in this country. Just try to get a passport or some travel documents. You'll see. Or better yet, go try to get yourself baptized in the Russian Orthodox faith." Meyer broke into laughter, elbowing his nephew playfully.

Chaim slumps in the wagon seat, evidencing anxiety. "Alright," says Meyer, letting up on him. "Don't worry. You're not *really* a momzer. You're a momzer only *technically* under the government's regime. A momzer is a child born of a married woman by a man to whom she's not married, or a child born of an incestuous relationship. Your parents were unrelated and they were married to each other, even before you were born. So you're kosher. You're not a bastard. You simply don't have a birth certificate. It's a mere technicality."

But Chaim indicates dissatisfaction with this answer. Looking unappeased, he sits up and whines, "But why don't I have a birth certificate? I have heard that each year on the Czar's birthday people can go to the authorities and receive favors correcting legal matters. So why doesn't my father go? I've heard about this birth certificate thing before, and I've heard my mother ask him to go apply for one for me when the Czar's birthday comes, so why doesn't he go?"

"What? You want to be baptized," Meyer laughs?

"No—I don't want to be baptized."

"So what is it then? If your father was planning to send you away from the country, he'd get you a birth certificate,"

"No, that's not it either. It's because what's right-- what's right is right! I should have a birth certificate like everyone else. So why doesn't he get me one?"

"Ah, because my brother Eliezer is very wise," says Meyer. "He is afraid that if he goes and applies for a birth certificate for you, it will subject you to conscription into the army, and the Russian army is no place for a Jewish boy to be."

"But what if I want to be in the Russian army," Chaim retorts petulantly?

Meyer pulls up on the reins abruptly bringing the wagon to a stop. He looks sternly at his nephew with uncomfortable surprise in his eyes. "What are you—a *mishugina* (crazy person)? Nobody wants to be in the Russian army—especially not this Russian army! If you don't get shot by a Menshevik, you'll get shot by a Bolshevik, and if that doesn't happen, your commander will have you beaten for something, or some Cossack will come along and try to kick your teeth in because you're a Jew. In this army you never even have to see a foreign enemy to get yourself killed! And the way things are going in the Russian Empire right now, even if you never run into an enemy soldier while you're in the army you'll probably be killed. I've heard that they send Jews off to wars without even giving them rifles. That's probably what would happen to you. How would you like that?"

"Uncle, don't you think you're exaggerating? Why would they even want me in the army if they weren't going to give me a gun? They'd just have to feed me and give me a uniform to wear, and what good would I be to them?"

"Intelligence, my boy. Intelligence. They're always saying we Jews are so crafty and smart. That's what they'd use you for, intelligence."

Chaim broke into one of his uncontrollable fits of laughter. "Intelligence? That's not what intelligence is Uncle. It's not smarts. In the army, intelligence is spying, and spies still need guns. I think you're just being unpatriotic when you say things like that."

"Oy, so now he's a patriot," Meyer replies. "Next thing, he'll be a patriot who wants to get himself baptized. *Veysmere!* (woe is me!).

"Just teasing, uncle. I don't want to be in the Russian

army. Hah!—Got you back though, didn't I?" Again
Chaim gave out with that infectious laugh he was to have all
his life.

"So what did you learn today Chaim? At least you
learned what a momzer is and what it isn't—at least
technically speaking. So don't be so sensitive. Ok?"

Aha! So this is where it comes from, I dream! *He
learned it from his uncle. Harkening back to my youth, I
remember how all my life, my father has jokingly belittled
me without meaning to, and if I protest he says, 'Don't be so
sensitive. At least you learned something. Didn't you?'* Pa
was just kidding, but he didn't realize his kidding was taken
to heart and it really hurt, making me feel stupid and small.
To him, his teasing me was a sign of love, a very stunted
sign, but nonetheless, a showing of love—in his mind.

Suddenly a brick hits the side of the wagon—then
another. The goats become jittery, scraping their hoofs on
the floor of the cargo box and bleating like sheep. Victor
rears as best he can within his rig, but the horse evener
prevents his standing on his hind legs. Kasha struggles to
pick up the forward pace. A gaggle of men run out from a
side-street, taking after the wagon and begin boarding it. In
the intersection ahead of us two horses appear with rifle
holding riders wearing crossed bullet belts across their
chests. Meyer is forced to control the melee by rearing back
on the reigns, bringing the horses to an abrupt stop.

"Well, what have we here," asks one of the Cossack
horsemen in Russian?

"Jews with goats," shouts the other.

"Get out of here," Chaim yells in Russian as he turns
around toward the back of the wagon in a rage. One of the
thugs answers by bashing him in the face. Another grabs
Meyer's buggy whip and begins beating Meyer.

"Grab their goats and let's go," someone shouts as he
opens the back gate of the buckboard. "Davai, davai, davai!"
(Come on, come on, come on!) Quickly the goats exit the

wagon and are driven off by the gang of thieves. The two Cossacks in front of the wagon accompany them on horseback, yelling back over their shoulders, "Cmert'na vse Evrei!" (Death to all Jews!)

Chaim is holding his bloody face in his hands as he watches his uncle jump down to the street to calm the horses by grabbing their bridles. Meyer's forehead is bleeding from the buggy whip and he's breathless. His hat has been knocked from his head, revealing his black yamulka and his coat is torn at the shoulder.

"Why, Uncle—why?" Chaim cries. "Those men are pigs. I want them to die. *Sviniah, sviniah*—pigs!

"Maybe another pogrom is starting," Uncle Meyer responds. "Chaim, remember! You must never speak to a Russian the way you did, no matter what he is doing, or trying to do to you. Never show disrespect for the *goyim* that way. You will only wind up getting beaten. They have clubs. They have knives, sometimes even guns or swords. You have nothing with which to defend yourself except your mind and your quick wits."

"It's not fair, Uncle! Why should they be able to treat us this way just because we're Jews? We are also Russians. I will defend myself—I will, with both my mind and my body. Look, I am already bigger than many of them."

Enough with the being poor put-upon, always discriminated against Jews, and with the deluding of ourselves that we are smarter than our oppressors I dream. Where has this arrogance gotten us so far? It's time to give all that up—to stop feeling sorry for ourselves but also that we're better. I can't tell if this is my thought or Chaim's thought in the dream. It's as if I'm having a secondary dream. But in my murky state of mind the primary dream suddenly intervenes to overtake it.

"Many Russians don't really feel we're Russians, Chaim," Meyer opines. To them we're unlike any of the other nationalities they've conquered to make up the Russian

Empire. To them, we're just *traifeneh smuts.* That's right. They think of us as forbidden dirt,-- thieves, like they think of the Gypsies. That's why we need our own country, our own state—in Palestine. You have heard me talk about this many times before. As Jews we need our own homeland, our own government, our own army. Only then can we be safe in our homes and on the streets."

"But for now we are living here in Kherson Uncle, and I think of it as my home, the home of my family and their family before them. What shall we do in the here and now?"

"Now, in the here and now, that is, with no goats left to take to market, let us turn around and head home for the day," Meyer says. "It will never get any better in this country for us. Never!"

When they arrive home, the Zelitzer household is abuzz. The Shertok family is visiting, having brought their two daughters and their 8-year-old son Moishe along. Boris and Eva Shertok (later to become named "Sharett") are both Zionists who are preparing to move their family to Ottoman Palestine. Only a delay in their receipt of the necessary travel documents through the Turkish Caliphate is holding them from leaving. Their upcoming journey is the most important thing on their minds at the moment, although not as important as they could ever have imagined. How could they have known that their little Moishe would someday become the leader of a country that does not even exist at this time? Moshe Sharett, the second prime minister of Israel.

Eliezer greets Chaim and Meyer in despair when they return to the Zelitzer house. 'It's trouble for certain,' he says. "It's another pogrom. Another pogrom has started."

All over the city Jewish shops and businesses are being ransacked. Word travels quickly of the plundering, but there are no stories of any deaths so far. According to Boris Shertok, the pogrom has started because a young Jew from Kherson named Lev Davidovich Bronstein, who calls

himself Leon Trotsky, has given a speech somewhere outside
Russia calling for working people in all the countries of the
world to seize social, economic and political power and ally
themselves as the proletariat with the peasantry to take over
everything. The czar doesn't like this. The Russian
bourgeoisie doesn't like it, and neither do the czar's
henchmen, the Cossacks. Hence, the latest pogrom.

"This is just another example of why we're going to
Palestine," Boris Shertok declares. "Here, it's not enough
that the Russians should blame us for everything that's
already wrong with the country. No—in addition, someone
has a new political idea they don't like, and if he happens to
be Jewish, they blame us all for that too. That is why we
need a complete break with the past—a new country of our
own on a different continent. Things will never change
here—never! Palestine will be the only place we can live in
peace. It is our ancient homeland, and not only that, but it is
a country without people waiting for a people, like us,
without a country."

Chaim smirks. He doesn't understand any of this, least
of all what this Trotsky's theory has to do with the Jews. "If
they don't like what this Trotsky has to say," Eliezer argues
to anyone who happens to be listening, "why take it out on
the Jews? We aren't peasants from the farms who've been
given land after serfdom was outlawed. Also, we aren't the
unskilled laborers known as the proletariat. So this Trotsky
person is not speaking to us or for us. Rather, we are
workers who actually own their own means of production,
like Meyer's shop, or my dry-goods business.

"We may be poor, or we may be wealthy, but we own
our own means of making a living, and we are contractors
and salesmen, not employees. The proletariat are not like us.
They are   unskilled laborers who own nothing, descendants
of peasants who did not stay on the land after the abolition of
serfdom, but rather went into the cities to look for work.
And today, they are dependent on foreign investors, factory

owners, Russian industrialists and government run businesses for their jobs. We Jews depend only on ourselves."

Chaim also could not understand his uncle's obsession with Zionism, or the Shertok's yearning to move to Palestine. What could a land without a people have to offer that Kherson did not? There was nothing in that land! True, here in Russia, maybe Jews weren't treated like the other Russians, but at least Chaim had the Yiddish stories of his favorite author, Sholem Aleichem, to read in his own Yiddish language. The cheerfulness of Aleichem's characters in the face of adversity provided Chaim with a coping mechanism for his own difficult life. What he did not realize was that Sholem Aleichem was also devoted to the cause of Zionism.

Even with incidents like the one he and his uncle had just undergone, Chaim, as a boy, is content to enfold himself within the culture surrounding him, a life of *"Yiddishism,"* so to speak, encapsulated within the Ukrainian city of Kherson at the southern tip of the Russian Empire. He is planning to go nowhere, reaching for no new political theory, dreaming no dream of the future. His view did not change even when his uncle once took him to Kiev for a meeting of *Hovevei Zion*, a group that was one of the forerunners and foundation builders of modern Zionism. There he was introduced to the most prominent member of the organization, Solomon Naumovich Rabinovich, aka, Sholem Aleichem, himself.

FOUR

"Nothing begets friendship so readily as trouble."
Sholem Aleichem

Startled awake by my mother calling from downstairs, "Lester, Lester, please come down," I fight my way back to consciousness. Ma is very excited. "Michale Narodnicki is here. He wants to see you," she shouts.

And then comes another sound, Narodnicki's hoarse, very nasal voice cheerfully alternating between Russian and English, "Yes, Lazer. Lazer —*Idti izdis* Come down here."

Like a leitmotif, Michale's voice, jars me toward the thought once again of how much I detest my name. Yes, as I always knew, my mother lied to me. Years ago upon asking her the reason she named me Lester, which I hate, she responded, "I was lying in the hospital after you were born, in a room with a woman who spoke English very well. She asked me, 'what did you call your baby,' and I told her I had not yet picked a name, but I want to give him a good English name. What do you think is a good English name? 'Well, I've always liked Lester,' she said. So, you are Lester. She was a lovely lady from a town called Leicester, England."

Now it's confirmed that Mom has lied because she knew I hated things reminding me my parents were immigrants. Here is my father's oldest living friend from Russia calling me Lazer, not in Russian or English, but in Yiddish. My parents' best immigrant friends from Hungary, the Blooms, also have always called me Lazer. It's not a Hungarian name. It's a Yiddish name. Come to think of it, I could tell my mother and father were referring to me when they argued in Yiddish, not wanting me to know what they were talking about. They would use the name Lazer in place of Lester. "Lazer this—and Lazer hat."

Learning at the funeral, for the first time, that my grandfather's name was Eliezer Ha Levi, I could put two and two together. I am not named Lester because of the English woman in the hospital. They named me Eliezer after my grandfather—Eliezer Ha Levi, which is the Yiddish equivalent of Lester. Lazer is the Yiddish nickname for Eliezer. My brother's name is Benjamin, the same thing in Yiddish or English, and when my parents argued in Yiddish about him, they always used his Yiddish/Hebrew/English name—Ben, or Binyamin.

Well, what does it matter anyways, I think? Michale Narodnicki is here, and I've got to get my butt downstairs.

Narodnicki is wearing a long black coat over a vest. He's a very thin man. Beneath his vest is a white, widely pin-striped shirt, slightly yellowing at the collar, which is buttoned all the way up without any tie over the top button. Atop his slender nose are his wire-rimmed glasses, actually a pinc nez, as always, with a thin silver chain hanging down and around his neck to save the glasses from falling to the floor. Narodnicki's family, like Pa's is from the middle to lower middle class in Kherson in which his father was a bootmaker. He is, I should say "was," my father's oldest living friend from Russia. Growing up, I had seen him from time to time, and today he looks the same as always—like an emaciated Stalin with a thick mustache whose equally thick hair is white instead of black. Narodnicki is neither an intellectual nor a Jew as the affectation of the a pince nez perched across his nose might suggest.

My father and Michale became friends when both of their lives suddenly and drastically changed. According to Michale, they met while being drafted into the Navy of Czar Nicholas II at the same time, and they became friends when they first reported for duty on the same day. (No matter to

the navy, Pa had no birth certificate, as I had dreamed.)
Michale describes the naval station at Kherson where they
reported as being very crowded with conscripts, and with
those failing or refusing to report for duty being rounded up
in wagons by the Cossacks and just dumped inside the door.

"Who knew we were about to embark on the greatest
adventure of our lives together when we met," he tells the
people who came to the house to console us after the
funeral?

A small man at 87, Michale was still healthier than a lot
of men half his age. He had travelled to Cleveland from
Detroit by himself to pay honor to my father, and he was
staying with his niece and her family. After coming to
America, he became a streetcar driver, then a bus driver, and
then a manager for the Detroit Transportation Authority.
Remarkably, with the passage of time, he and my father
happened upon each other in the "new world," to which they
had unexpectedly come together, and they were able to keep
up their relationship through the years.

"Chaim was 15," Narodnicki said as he began his tale
about their time together in the Russian Navy. "It is 1904.
Chaim tells me about his father's ruse of not getting him a
birth certificate in order to help him evade the draft. At the
time, I consider this to be a most unpatriotic thing to do, and
typical of the screeds I had often read, but rejected, about the
Jews. I don't let it bother me much though, because
obviously Eliezer Ha Levy Zelitzer's plan has failed. Chiam
Zelitzer has received the same treatment as me. We are both
going to have our lives interrupted by navy service.

"It seems the czar's officers don't care who was born
legally, or who was born illegally, and it also becomes quite
obvious they know where all young men of draft age live
without searching the government administrative records.
Besides, I have my own grievance with government in St.
Petersburg, and it is greatly occupying my mind. St.
Petersburg doesn't seem to care much about families like

mine that are slowly sinking away from the middle class into the industrial class of workers because they lack any connection with the powers that be in the government. This fact has become evident because the army refuses to contract with my father to make boots for its soldiers. The politics of my family are just wrong, or some such thing like that. Thus, the bureaucrats in St. Petersburg are doing their best to consign us to the proletariat without a business of our own.

"In any event there is nothing to be done about that now because war is about to break out between Russia and Japan over who controls Manchuria and Korea. Chaim tells me he had no idea such a war was going to happen. But I know why that is. He can't read the Russian Newspapers, and the Yiddish newspapers don't care what is going on in Korea and Manchuria. But I, who had a Russian education, on the other hand, at least know some of the things that are happening in the world at large because I am not living inside the Yiddish bubble in which Chaim has been reared.

"I know at the time that the Russian Empire needs warm water ports. The only ones it has are at Kronstadt in the Baltic, Kherson and Odessa on the Black Sea, and Murmansk in the North. All the rest are ice-bound for part of the year. Specifically, I know from reading the gazette that Russia needs a warm water port known as Port Arthur, which happens to be in Manchuria.

"I also know that at the time, Theodore Roosevelt, the President of the United States, is assiduously working to make himself the arbiter of the growing dispute between Japan and Russia over this port and the mediator of the imperial ambitions of both of the countries. Japan wants Port Arthur. In fact, she wants all of Manchuria. So the dispute has exploded into the Russo-Japanese War of 1904-05, which suddenly, for no reason important to us becomes the problem of Michale Narodnicke and Chaim ben Eliezer Ha Levi Zelitzer. .

"The war is largely a set of naval battles in which the

Japanese eviscerate the Russian Navy at Port Arthur on the coast of Manchuria. Then the "soldiers of the sun" defeat the two-headed Russian Eagle in the largest land battle up until that time in the world at a place called "Mukden." The battle is larger than any that has been fought before, even in America's Civil War."

Narodnicki is telling a story I had never heard. Pa and he were drafted as *Matrocii* (Seamen), and shipped off to Vladivostok on Russia's east coast to the ships that were waiting there to defend that city, which was the eastern-most port of the Russian Empire and its only outlet to the Pacific Ocean. The only other harbor Russia controlled on the Pacific was Port Arthur in Manchuria which Russia had taken over from China. It was a time of great turmoil, with many Russians believing their government should be taking better care of the people at home instead of fighting a far off war.

As if to apologize for his earlier statement that Chiam's father was not patriotic, Narodnicki then adds, "Despite political tensions at home, many Russian Jews served patriotically and loyally in this war, which Russia lost badly," Then he looks at me and declares, "Unfortunately, your father was not among such patriots. Nor was I. We both deserted."

I was aghast. I had never heard about this. Actually, I had heard practically nothing about my father's time in Russia. I had just comfortably accepted the concept that he was an immigrant who came to the United States because things were better here than in Russia. After all, that seemed to be the story of the parents of many others with whom I was going to school. Nobody ever talked about what went on with their parents back in Russia or Eastern Europe.

"You mean my father was a deserter? I gasped."

"Relax *malchik* (boy). That is a good thing, not a bad thing. Here's how it went. Eliezer Ha Levi cared little for the empire's honor. Rather, he saw Chaim's conscription as an opportunity, once and for all, to get him away from all the pogroms plaguing the Ukraine. As for me, I could never understand the vicious anti-Semitism of what seemed like almost every non-Jew in the Ukraine. I read the anti-Semitic stories in the newspapers. I heard bad things about the Jews when I went to the Cathedral of St. Catherine in Kherson. I listened to some of my family members going on and on about the Jews. But what I didn't realize until the war, was that things were so bad for the Jews in Ukraine that they were leaving the Russian Empire in droves for the United States and other destinations to avoid all the Jew hating.

"I also didn't realize that leaving took money and established relatives in the U. S. or another country who could vouch for and support an immigrant. The Zelitzer family was not wealthy by any means, especially after paying Chaim's sister Pauline's immigration passage to America via the Black Sea and the Mediterranean, paying a few bribes to people in the United States who offered to act as her sponsor and donating money to the Jewish Agency for what passed for her care after getting her through Ellis Island in New York. The family had only a few things of value left, and they were prepared to give up the rest of what they had to get more of the family out of the country and to America in any way they could. Chaim, being a teenager at the time, of course didn't know much about his immediate family's plans or desires. Oh, but let me not get ahead of myself in this tale.

"Here's how the story unfolded. Chaim and I are shipped East to Vladivostok across Siberia on the Trans-Siberian Railway. We are supposed to meet up with the Russian Second Pacific Squadron, originally called the Baltic Fleet, that's sailing all the way from Krondstadt on the Baltic Sea, around the Cape of South Africa; and into the Arabian Sea to the Indian Ocean and on, to the East China Sea. They can't use the Suez Canal because our ships would have been sitting ducks there. At the time Britain and Japan are allies.

"Can you imagine being encased in a steel hauled battle cruiser for seven months with ship rats, coal, oil and disease? That's how long the trip takes by sea, and that's what other Russian sailors did. They sailed all of the way out of the Baltic past all of the Scandinavian countries, down along the coast of France, Spain and Portugal, across the entrance to the Mediterranean Sea to West Africa, and then to South Africa, and up past Madagascar to India, and from there to China.

"At least the navy has the good sense to avoid that arduous journey for us by shipping us across Siberia on the newly built Trans-Siberian Railroad to meet up with the squadron in Vladivostok. The train passage through Siberia, however, is plenty tough for us," Narodnicki rasps, "because the Russian Navy is now down to pressing into service untrained conscripts, as well as sullen reservists, mingled with troublemakers and agitators, lunatics, drunkards, invalids, and potential mutineers, all of whom are traveling with us. We all travel across Siberia together in filthy box cars with only a small stove for heat and two open latrines at the head of the cars and a small door in the back that can be opened for ventilation.

"Chaim is quite a big fellow, so I stick very close to him during the voyage for the physical protection he can provide me. I sleep next to him as our rail car, which has wooden sleeping racks with hay, tiered up three levels high along the walls, rolls eastward across the permafrost on the trans-Siberian tracks, and I always try to sit near him on the floor during daylight hours. This causes me soon to notice that he never takes off his rucksack, and that he always carefully places his hat in his belt when he sleeps. 'Why do you never let your pack out of your sight,' I ask him? He refuses to tell me.

"I later learn his secret when a thug from Odessa accuses me of cheating at cards and throws me up against the wall of our box car. Swinging into action, Chaim kicks the man between the legs, yelling at him to leave me alone."

"'Jew,' the man shouts pulling out a knife. 'Now I will carve you up,' and he lunges toward Chaim, who has positioned himself at the doorway in the back end of the car as it rolls along. Chaim throws open the door and the man goes hurtling out of the coach onto a platform beyond, at which time Chaim follows him outside and proceeds to kick him off the platform of the moving train. There is a scream. For a moment, all we can hear is the breeze coming in the open door and the clickety-clack of the wheels as they move along the tracks. Then Chaim comes back in alone, and all the passengers begin applauding. 'How did you know to do that? I ask?'"

"'When he called me Jew, it reminded me of what my uncle once told me—that the *goyim* have guns and knives and all I have to defend myself with is quick wits, so that's what I did—used quick wits,' he says. 'I knew that when the man lunged at me, he would just keep going and fly outside if I stepped aside and opened the door for him. Then he lets go with the longest, loudest laughing I've ever heard.' It lasts so long that it becomes infectious. All the others in the car begin laughing too. 'Da, the one thing you Jews have going for you is your smarts,' somebody yells."

"The other thing I can never forget is that during the fight, pieces of silverware had spewed out of Chaim's rucksack and clanked down on the floor of the coach car. Later, he tells me the silverware had been sewn into his army issue pack, and his uncle's tiny machine shop was sold off for precious stones to be hidden under the seams of his military cap.

"'For what purpose was this done,' I ask. 'Why are you carrying silverware and jewels with you?'

"'Don't tell anybody, but it's for my escape,' he confides, whispering, 'This journey will be the most important in my life. I'm leaving the navy and running away to America once we reach Vladivostik, and my family has given me these things to help me with trip.

'You're crazy,' I tell him. 'Do you know what the penalty for desertion is? 'Don't you know there's a vast ocean between where we're going and America?'

'I know the penalty is a firing squad,' he says, 'and I know how far away America is, but I'll make it. I have to make it, because I think that one day my uncle will convince my father to uproot the family and go to live in Palestine, and I don't want to live there."

"I fall asleep," says Narodnicki, "as I'm beginning to think how truly crazy Chaim is. But as the story goes on, the whole thing begins to seem not so crazy."

"How so," I ask? "It seems to me like they were all pretty nuts back then—Pa, his father, Pa's Uncle Meyer, and Pa's mother. Of course, I didn't know any of them, so it would be imprudent for me to judge them. But their plan to get my father out of Russia seems pretty risky, and the probability of success seems non-existent."

"Well, here's what in fact happened," says Narodcki. He then explains the last big battle of the Russo-Japanese War of 1904-05 entailed the defeat of the Russian Pacific Squadron outside Vladivostok in the battle of Tsushima Straits. "Even though he couldn't swim, your father served in that battle as a Russian seaman aboard the battleship Suvarov, which carried Rear Admiral Zinovy Petrovitch Rozhestvensky. I was assigned to the same ship.

"Your father's job as a seaman is that of mechanic in the main engine room. Normally, this keeps him below decks. I worked on deck doing regular seaman's work, but in times of battle, my job was that of loader of the two twelve inch 40 caliber guns mounted in the electrically operated center pivot turret set on the fore-deck. Each of these guns fired a 730-pound shell at a muzzle velocity of approximately 2500 feet per second, to a range of 12,000 yards. So naturally they were prime targets for the Japanese warships. Our first engagement, after entering the Sea of Japan, turns out to be the Battle of Tushima. Our main turret is hit and put out of action shortly after the start of the battle.

"Soon, the <u>Suvarov</u> is dealing with a huge fire on board. Your father is ordered above deck to help us fight the fire, and there we run into each other. Together we watch our sister ship, the <u>Oslybya</u>, sink. It's the first of quite a few Russian vessels to go to the bottom on that day—in all, five battleships, four cruisers, and five torpedo boats. When all this begins happening, Chaim looks at me and I at him.

'What are we going to do,' I ask?

"'We're going to get out of here as soon as we can,' he says. Then we hear word that Admiral Rozhestvensky is badly wounded, and he is going to be evacuated off our ship. Suddenly, there is a terrible crushing sound and we hear the horrible metallic yawn of screeching metal splitting open as a torpedo slams into the side of the <u>Suvarov</u> just below the water line. Within seconds another one explodes into us.

"A repetitive strum, strum, strum commences as the ship begins to crack up. The rivets are unfastening and the welds are squealing open, but the propeller keeps turning, making the strumming sound. Within 10 minutes the <u>Suvarov</u> begins to list. The water-tight compartments below are too damaged to prevent the ship from sinking, and it begins to go down nose first. The incessant strumming continues even more loudly as the prop breaks the surface of the water.

"Chaos is reigning, and amidst all this, Admiral Roshestvensky has to be transferred to the destroyer <u>Buiyny</u>. Everyone seems focused on that. It is then that Chaim seizes his moment. He runs below decks just long enough to grab his rucksack and service hat, and then he resurfaces.

'Davai, davai Narodnicki,' he yells. 'We are going with the admiral, getting off this boat right now. Follow me.'

"We run to the seaward side of the sinking ship as she lists to the starboard and jump into the admiral's launch with the other seamen there who are readying to motor the officer staff and the Admiral to the destroyer Buiyny. In all the confusion, nobody notices us. Or if they do, they don't care we're there because they're too busy saving their own lives. It's the same old Russian hierarchy of aristocratic class preference at work again, only this time in the navy. *Save the aristocracy and to hell with the common man. He doesn't even exist at times like these.*

"The launch reaches the Buiyny just as the Suvarov was going under. The Buiyny escapes to Vladivostok. When the Buiyny reaches the dock at Vladivostok, we learn that the remnant of the Russian Navy had raised a white table cloth and surrendered to the Japanese back at Tsushima. It's over. Russia's exhausted. She's lost the war. Two thirds of her fleet is destroyed. What was left sailed to Manilla. Fifteen hundred of her sailors have been interned by the Japanese; 4,380 Russians are dead; and 5,917 are prisoners.

According to Narodnicki, Chaim and he took advantage of the confusion over the massive defeat to desert. They would somehow get to America. They stole some civilian clothes from a store; hid in a warehouse overnight; and, the next morning they began a trek for miles, walking from Vladivostok to Harbin in Manchuria. From there, they stowed away in a box car on the newly constructed Chinese Eastern Railway for 550 miles to Port Arthur in Manchuria, which is now in the hands of the Japanese who had earlier crushed the Russian fortifications there and sunk half of the first Russian Pacific fleet bottled up in the harbor.

"We hadn't eaten anything in three days. It seemed our choices had run out now. Port Arthur is in the hands of the Japanese; our prospects don't look good if we surrender to the Japanese.

"It was then that I was able to add a suggestion that was valuable to our endeavors," Narodnicki said. "I knew from reading the Russian newspapers that the British had sided with the Japanese in this war and that they were in Port Arthur in order to protect British interests there. But the

Englishmen would be more understanding of Russian sailors than would the Japanese because England had not actually fought in the war and because Englishmen and Russians were both European. So in Port Arthur, Chaim and I surrender ourselves to the British Consulate, even though the British are allies of Japan."

FIVE

"Even to be unlucky you have got to have a little luck."
-- Sholem Aleichem

"It wasn't easy," Narodnicki continues. "Neither your father nor I could speak a word of Chinese, Japanese or English. Because of our desertion, we were now men without a country, refugees completely dependent on the British and what the British decided to do with us. If they sent us back to Russia, most certainly we would wind up in a gulag somewhere in Siberia as deserters working our lives out or worse. If they turned us over to the Japanese, who knew what would happen. We might be taken back to Japan and interned there in a prisoner of war camp. Or they might decide to trade us for Japanese prisoners, in which case we would eventually wind up in a gulag if word of our desertion got out. For the moment, they jailed us in the British stockade at Port Arthur.

"I became morose, stuck up there in northeast China with nowhere to go, even if I could have gotten out of that British jail. The weather was depressing. The scenery was depressing. The situation was depressing. Everything was foreign, right down to the food they gave us to eat. Chaim, on the other hand, never gave up hope. 'We will get out of here. You'll see. Something will happen and we'll get to North America. Think of it this way Narodnicki. Now that we've crossed Siberia, we're already half way there.' It's true. Chaim had a sense of humor, and he was always positive but it didn't help. We had no plan.

"There was one other Russian imprisoned with us at

38

Port Arthur, an officer who had been arrested by the
Japanese when the city fell. His name was Gulatov. At the
conclusion of the battle, Russian officers were given the
choice of either going into prisoner of war camps with their
men or being given parole on the promise of taking no
further part in the war. Of course Gulatov chose parole But
then he violated his parole by trying to lead Russian
prisoners he had freed, off to fight in the Battle of Mukdon,
which was about to occur north of Port Arthur. The British
were now holding him as an accommodation to the Japanese
until he could be shipped to a prisoner of war camp in Japan.
The point is, he could speak and understand English. Thus,
he became our only connection with the people with whom
we dealt at Port Arthur. Other than that, he was a horrible
man who wanted to be paid for translating for us. This used
up almost all the silverware your father was still carrying.

"The Russian officer's translation services also helped
reveal to us that our British jailor, Sergeant Helmsley, was a
vicious man who loved to entertain himself by tormenting
us. He would say that the British High Commissioner on
Refugees was coming to Port Arthur and wanted to talk with
us. We would wait and wait for this with the highest
anticipation that negotiations would occur with him that
would somehow lead to our freedom. After all he was a
European like us, not an Asian, and the British had no great
love for Russia after the Crimean War. Surely he would be
responsive to our requests for asylum in the West. But he
would never come. He never showed up.

"Then we found out that he wasn't coming, and that in
fact, there was no British High Commissioner of Refugees.
Instead, Sergeant Helmsley said that in the morning Japanese
officers would be at the Consulate to take us away. They
came alright, but instead of taking us away, they put us in
bamboo cages where we had to sit all day without any water.
The cages were only four feet high. The point of this
confinement was to make us talk about the size and

weaponry of the Russian forces at Muckdon, about which we
knew nothing. Over and over, we would tell them the
Russians at Muckdon are army and we are navy. We knew
nothing about the army's maneuvers. These answers only
resulted in beatings which were administered with wooden
sticks.

Sergeant Helmsley would say he didn't like Russians
very much, especially dumb ones, and then he would spit in
our food as he delivered it to us. He was an effeminate little
man whom your father once referred to as the *"fagela"* (bird
in Yiddish), and when Helmsley asked Gulatov what that
meant, the officer told him he didn't know, that it wasn't
Russian. So Helmsley made us clean all the toilets in the
Consulate building until we translated the word for him,
which we never did. Instead, we told him it was little more
than a Ukrainian term of endearment for one's "boss."

"When we weren't being tormented or tortured, we just
languished in this British jail, where we met many drunken
Canadian soldiers of fortune who were drying out for the
night in the jailhouse. They had volunteered to come over
and fight for the Japanese. When the war ended, they ended
up drinking on the streets of Port Arthur and they were
thrown into prison to dry out until transportation back to
Canada could be arranged for them. But arranging
transportation back to Canada was no easy fete. The British
just didn't care about them, and the Canadian government
took the position that their leaving Canada to fight in the war
was not a part of any Canadian government program, and
they were merely on a lark of their own. Why should
Canadian taxpayers foot the bill for bringing them back to
Canada? Many of them had to somehow find a way to pay
their own passage back through various means.

"As things turned out, it was the Canadian government's
mistreatment of its own citizens that resulted in our finally
getting out of that British jail and to North America. It was a
circumstance nobody could have planned on. It was also a

circumstance that confirmed my faith in God to this day. The Canadian inmates of the jail were—I don't know how you would say it—they called themselves a 'hail and hardy" bunch, and they were always friendly to us. One day, one of them teased, 'Hey you Russkis. You want to be Canuks? You want to come back to Canada with us? All you have to do is sign a contract to work on one of the railroads there for two years without any pay, and they'll take care of your passage to Canada, feed you while you work for them and put a roof over your head. It may be a tent at times, but at least it won't be raining down on your head. Of course you have to not mind being serfs to the railroad for a while.'

"Most of the Canadians scorned this idea as being almost a form of indentured slavery just to get back home to their loved ones. They preferred to wait for the Canadian government to bring them home properly. But to Chaim and me, the idea seemed like a saving grace.

"Chaim used up the rest of the jewels and silverware sewn into his hat and into his backpack to pay for the translation of the contracts the Canadian Railroad required in order to employ us and pay for our passage. Eventually, we wound up selling ourselves as contract laborers to the Canadian Northern Railway Company of Manitoba for two years in return for passage across the Pacific Ocean to British Columbia, and then on to Edmonton Alberta.

"I shall never forget the kindness your father showed to help me with this in getting to America. He didn't have to do it, you know. He didn't have to spend the little stash he'd carried all the way from Kherson on me as well as himself. He didn't have to pay Gulatov to translate my contract as well as his.

"Thus," concluded Michale Narodnicki, "your father did not enter North America like all the other *"greenie"* Jews— via Ellis Island. He was one of a handful who came via British Columbia through Canada. And I came with him, in the bottom of a Canadian freighter.

David Selcer

"The hold of that ship where we bunked was filled with rats and stench. All of the other passengers down there with us were Chinese coolies. It was so bad that each morning the crew didn't have to wait for us to crawl up the ladder to the deck. We were always waiting there at the top as they opened the hatch, and we would run out on deck to breath huge swaths of the sea breeze. The passage across took two weeks, and in those two weeks it seemed like we cleaned every brass fitting in the wheel house and painted every air vent above the deck. We also painted the ship's funnels.

"When we finally saw Canada, it reminded us of Siberia. There seemed to be no beautiful cities like Odessa there, and no sophisticated places like Kiev. Vancouver, with its multitude of streetcars, horse drawn carriages and wagons was mildly reminiscent of Kiev, but that was about it. Otherwise there was only raw weather, raw people, snow and 'Indians,' not from India. There were no towns with streets "paved with gold" like we had heard New York was supposed to be—although we were told there had recently been a gold rush around Victoria Island. Mostly, Canada seemed to be a country of forests, mountains, snow and more snow, and except in Vancouver and Victoria, every structure was made out of wood.

. . .

Narodnicki wasn't finished yet. He still had stories to tell about their time in Canada, and everybody in the room was stll interested. The ladies in the kitchen brought in some tea and cakes for him. I winced as I watched him place a cube of sugar between his front teeth and suck the tea back through them. It was like watching my own father. Just a Russian thing I guess—drinking tea like that.

Then he carried on with his story. "Do you want to know how Chaim became Hyman," he asked? Everyone nodded yes.

"While laboring to build a tunnel near Edmonton, Canada his foreman, an Irish man who couldn't pronounce the guttural rough "ch" sound that marked the first syllable of his name, Chaim, changed his name to "Ayman," which the man supposed was the Irish equivalent of Chaim. Gradually, this became "Hyman," the name your Pa carried for the rest of his life.

"Building the railroad across Canada became real drudgery. Filling the roadbeds with rocks and gravel and then smoothing it was back breaking work, although there were steam-driven machines to help us with this. But then we had to set the ties by hand, and they were heavy, rough and smelly. Seating the ties was the hardest part because it was all shovel and rake work, again, totally by hand. After we put the ties in, twenty or so men would set each rail by hand. Spiking the rails to the ties with sledge hammers was the only part of the job everyone enjoyed, but that work was only for the bigger men. It wasn't for me, and not for the Chinese workers either.

"'Just watch Ayman mates,' the foreman used to yell. 'He can drive a spike true with just two swings of the hammer and you'll never see that rail move, no matter what comes across it.' Thus for a while, Hyman's nickname became 'Spike'.

"Then there's the story of how we both wound up coming to these great United States of America. As the railroad expanded, we moved eastward toward Ontario to help link it up with another railroad being built out of Quebec. By the time we reached Montreal in Quebec Province, we had fulfilled our two-year contracts with the Canadian Northern Railway. We had a little English by then, and it was getting better, but we quickly learned this would be of no avail in Montreal, where more people spoke French than English. 'I don't think I can learn French' Hyman said. 'Can you?'

David Selcer

" *'Nyet,'* I said, *'Ya ne chochu'* (No, and I don't want
to.) Bora *ya est Russki!* (I'm a Russian for god sakes).' So
we left the company, and we left Montreal, heading south to
the United States across the St. Lawrence River. Eventually,
we split up with Chaim, now Hyman, going back to Ontario
and crossing Lake Ontario to Rochester, New York and me
illegally crossing from Canada into Vermont near Lake
Champlain. In that part of the world all you had to do was
slip under some farmer's fence and you had crossed from
Canada to the United States. There were no Mounties up
there and no U.S. border patrol in Vermont. That's how I
did it. I walked through the Champlain Valley.

"Once you got over the border, it was pretty easy to get
yourself fake papers. All it took was money, and I had the
money they'd mustered me out of the railroad company with
when I left. The real problem for me was the language, but
that's a whole different story.

"Hyman crossed the border into Rochester with no
problem, as I later learned from him. He applied to enter the
United States through the Hebrew Immigration Society, and
they met him at the docks in Rochester and helped him to
cross legally into the U.S. every step of the way.

"We did not meet again until many years later, and then
it was only by chance. I moved to Detroit where I eventually
became a bus driver. Your father moved here to Cleveland,
but he had a relative in Detroit, one of two sisters he now
had living there. Once he was visiting her, and he just
happened to get on my bus. Thus, we met again. As we
used to say in Russia, 'God is always where you're not
looking for him.' I never expected to see Hyman again but I
am certain that our chance meeting on that day was
preordained in Heaven. We had been connected before for a
purpose that turned out to be the greatest thing that could
have happened in both our lives, leaving the Russian Empire
and becoming Americans. I never thought of doing such a
thing and it was impossible for me to foresee that I would

ever become an American. Hyman never doubted that we would make it to this country. He just had no plan to make it happen. It was not right that once the task was accomplished, we should just go our separate ways. Providence saw to it that we didn't, and we became fast friends once more.

"I can never forget your father. That is why I came here from Detroit for his funeral when his sister told me he died. I will never forget him. I can never forget those times we had together and what he did for me."

Tears faintly came to Michale's eyes, which he embarrassedly brushed away. As he got up to leave, Ma wrapped his coat around him and ushered him to the door.

"Hymie never forgot you either Michale Narodnicki," she said. "He spoke of you many times to me."

I watched out the front window as he left. His niece was waiting for him in a car. Once outside, the old Russian Orthodox man stood on the porch facing the street for a moment, and he crossed himself in that strange Cyrillic way the Eastern Orthodox do. Then he went down the steps and departed.

SIX

"Love is a taste of paradise."
--Sholem Aleichem

"After Mr. Narodnicki left, my mother continued my father's story. She, too, told of things I never knew or imagined. "It was literally a miracle." she said, "that the secret plan Eliezer Zelitzer had whispered to his son about getting out of Russia as he was leaving for his naval service, actually worked. Since the cost of immigration prohibited Chaim's departure on a proper steamship, his father encouraged him to leave his country by deserting the Russian Navy during the war. You could say, in a way, that instead of coming via a commercial steamer, he came via Russian battleship or a Canadian freighter."

"Other than that, the plan lacked any details beyond the secreting of valuables on Chaim's person. Can you imagine what his mother must have felt listening to her crazy husband encouraging their son to desert the navy as she sat in the house quietly sewing silverware and valuable jewelry into Chaim's rucksack?" Ma exclaimed. "It was outlandish. Once my poor Hymie reached Vladivostok, the plan for his escape was completely up to him. He was only a sixteen-year-old boy by then! Either his father was insensitive and insane, or he had the utmost confidence in his youngest son.

"It is by hook or by crook, mostly crook, that Hymie immigrated to the United states. He entered the country through Rochester, New York." She explained that after he crossed the border from Canada to the United Stated on Lake Ontario hidden under a tarp on fishing vessel, his first impression of this country was dominated by a large amusement park and resort along the shore at the harbor in

46

Rochester.

"Other than the clothes on his back, his only possessions at the time," she said, "were one remaining piece of silverware his mother had sewn into his rucksack for him back in Kherson, a soup ladle, and his termination papers showing he'd been a good employee of the Canadian Northern Railway Company of Manitoba. No matter," she added. "He he would become an American citizen in Rochester. By the way, I still have the soup ladle."

"His naturalization as an American citizen occurred, in part, because of the kind endeavors of a priest he met from the nearby sailors and seamen's home when he came ashore. Realizing that Hyman was a Jew, he placed him into the hands of the Hebrew Immigrant Aid Society (HIAS)."

Ma goes on to explain how HIAS arranged for Pa's naturalization as an American citizen, but not without great difficulty. His lack of a birth certificate almost proved fatal to the endeavor. Russia would not issue a certificate for him without his being present during the application process. Finally, his family was able to scrounge up his induction papers into the Russian Navy but that avenue began to fail when the immigration authorities asked for his discharge papers to go along with these. So, the tried and true method of obtaining government action had to be used: one more bribe was paid, and Chaim refiled his application for entry into the United States, this time under 'political refugee' status. It saved the day for him.

"His English was improving, but very slowly, and he yearned to speak Yiddish, or even Russian, when he met a fellow Jew, but everyone insisted on English. Although he continued to work on his English, HIAS arranged for him to attend naturalization classes given in Yiddish and to be tested orally in Yiddish rather than in writing in English.

"If you don't learn to speak English better than you can right now," his HIAS contact, Leonard Perlmutter, exhorted him, "you'll never make it in this country. This is the United

States—the great melting pot. Only English is spoken here. It's not like Canada, or like Russia where many different languages are spoken."

HIAS also finally got him a job. It wasn't much, but without any Western education, all he had to sell was the labor of his body. He worked for a scrap dealer, as the junk man who came to your back door collecting ruined pots and pans, used up tires and broken shovels and rakes. It was a lot different than what he'd done back in the Ukraine, but at least he got to drive a horse drawn wagon like his uncle's.

Otherwise, except for arranging the bribe, HIAS was unable to do much for Pa. They did, however, tell him to change his last name to Zeltzer because they thought it would be easier to pronounce. What HIAS couldn't do for him, however, the *shidkh* (Jewish matchmaker) could. The *shidkh* had plenty of young Jewish women in her portfolio waiting for her to make the right match. "One thing was for certain," said Ma. "Your father was always a handsome man, and there were a lot of new arrivals in Rochester looking for handsome men."

Ma smiled as she went on. She told us that Rochester was kind to Pa. She told us the story of a young Jewish "greenie," Hanna Golda, who had arrived in town from Galicia in Austria, via New York City, where she had been working in a sweatshop. A rabbi's daughter back in Austria, Hanna Golda was highly educated, speaking five languages and reading and writing in three of them. She could read books and newspapers in English; her mathematics ciphering was good, and she knew how to keep ledgers and accounts, as well as how to run a sewing machine. Not only that, but she had many relatives in Rochester, the Fogels, who were growing into one of the big well-known family names in the city. They were admired for their successful businesses, applauded for their beneficent donations of time and money to charities, and recognizable for their commerce with people outside the city. They also had two lawyers and a doctor among their family members.

But none of this did Hanna Golda much good. She was merely a distant relative from Europe to them, and the Fogels really didn't want her around. She had a big-name family to which she wanted to cling, but actually she was alone.

Hanna Golda's father, Rebbe Israel Fogel, was a *Hasidic* Jew who had managed to foist his daughter on his cousin's family in Rochester as the sponsor for her immigration to America by shaming them into vouching for her. "I've heard your family is so wealthy in America," he wrote to his cousin," and here we have so little. All you'll have to do is sign for her, and the authorities will see from your reputations that she won't be a burden on your country. But don't worry. Hanna can take care of herself when she gets there. She is very smart, and she is educated. It will cost you nothing."

The purpose of requiring a sponsor for immigration purposes is to be assured there is   somebody who will take care of the immigrant and help them get started in the New World. But the Fogels of Rochester really didn't want that responsibility. They were too busy making their way in America to pay Hanna Golda any attention. Nonetheless, they signed for her as her sponsor to get Rebbe Fogel off their backs.

To them, she was a nuisance, merely another mouth to feed, and they wanted to rid themselves of her. She again started sewing, this time dresses. The only difference was that instead of working in a sweatshop in New York City, she had a job in one of the sewing shops behind the Fogels' dry-goods store in Rochester. It soon became evident to her that she was not welcome.

Yes, Hannah Golda became my mother. She ended her sewing career in the sweatshops of America by wedding Pa and becoming Anne Zeltzer. When the *shidkh* brought Pa around to the Fogels, they jumped at the idea of marrying their Hanna to him. Let him take her off their hands, they thought. He was handsome. He was Jewish and he was young. Never mind that he had no real means of making a good living.

"Hyman, on the other hand, was very tentative with me," Ma notes, "and I with him. I was not looking for a man," she insisted. "Nothing in our lives had prepared either of us for what was about to happen."

"You are from Russia, I asked him in English, Ma said? "He failed to respond. *Vie goveritze parusski yazik,?*" "I tried again in Russian," she said, *"Akud vie v' Roccia?"* I asked. (You speak Russian? Where are you from in Russia?)

"His eyes lit up. '*Da*,' he replied. 'I can speak Russian. Ya c'*Kherson na Ukarainie*,' he added in stiff Russian. '*Ya Ivreski.*'"

"A Jew!" She responded, and she immediately began speaking to him in soft Yiddish tones.

"Da, Y*iddishe,*" Pa answered, as he comfortably switched from Russian into Yiddish, the true language of his past.

In this manner, they communicated with each other for two hours. He told her about the war and how he had deserted and come to Rochester through Canada. She talked of her days back in Galitzia as Rebbe Fogel's daughter, and how she knew how to *doven* (pray) at all the services—*mincha* (morning)—*musoff* (afternoon) and ma'*erev* (evening), but was never allowed to lead the prayers because she was a woman; how her father foresaw a great war coming to Europe; and how he had wanted to get her out of there for her safety. They discussed how Pa had nobody in the United States, except a sister somewhere in a place called Detroit, and how the Rochester Fogels were such a big family. Ma confessed she knew they really didn't want her around.

Soon Hyman began driving his junk wagon by the sewing shop where she worked behind the Fogels' dry goods establishment, even though it wasn't on his route, and there was no waste or junk to be had in the area. He did not, however, go into the shop, and Hanna Golda did not come out to greet him. That would have been improper. Instead, he would just waive from the wagon and she would smile at him from inside the shop. Hanna's cousin, Leon, watching this, one day ran out to Hyman because he was offended by the sight of the ugly junk wagon being behind his business so much.

"If you want to," he yelled, "just come by the house and take her for a picnic down to the river. But get this rattletrap and this smelly horse out of here and don't come back here with your rig! Don't bring it to the house either."

Hanna Golda, watching it all and listening from inside the shop, cried out, "Sunday, come this Sunday. I'll make sandwiches and some cold tea for us to take with us."

At the river, they sat by a tablecloth in the grass. They talked about their childhoods. Then Hyman sang to her and they began to compare Yiddish lullabies from their pasts. His favorite was *Shlof Mayn Kind* (Sleep My Child) because it was written by Shalom Aleichem. Hers was Rozhinkes Mit Mandlen (Raisins and Almonds) which they both new and sang together.

"You have a beautiful voice Hymie," she said--and when she called him Hymie, he let go with one of his kind, uncontrollable laughs.

Soon, a *shiddoch* was made, as the Rochester Fogels paid off the *shidkh* for the match, to get rid of Hanna Golda. They threw a modest wedding and reception, for the young couple, being sure to make it at an appropriate level, high enough to leave the neighbors talking about how good they had been to their young relative from the old country. But not too costly. Secretly they then sighed a sigh of relief, when they heard the crashing of the traditional glass breaking under Hymie's shoe, signifying that the wedding was complete. They yelled *Mazel Tov*, and then they presented the couple with a small sterling silver engraved tag containing both their old country names and their names for the future in America.

> To Chaim Hyman and Hanna Anne,
>   Congratulations on the occasion of your wedding.
>   1907.

In this way Chaim Zelitzer and Hannah Golda Fogel became Hyman and Anne Zeltzer.

"What does the breaking of the glass signify, Hymie," Anne asked that night when they were alone for the first time in Cousin Leon's house?

"I don't know," Hymie answered. "I don't think it has any meaning at all."

"Oh but it does," she insisted. "I think it's to remind us that life holds sorrow as well as joy."

And soon the sorrow of life manifested itself to them. The Fogels quickly learned that Hyman had no occupation with which to recommend himself but that of laborer. There was no call for machinists in Rochester and he had no education other than what he had learned at the synagogue in Kherson. There was nothing for him to do befitting the station of a Fogel in any of the Fogel enterprises. Pa scraped out a living delivering goods for them to their customers in their new horseless truck, which he slowly and very carefully learned to drive, and Ma had to go back to her sewing. Then, one day, Pa wrecked the truck, and Otto Fogel, the family patriarch, fired him. To make things worse, HIAS had washed its hands of Pa.

"Now what?" He asked his wife.

Instructed by the tradition of breaking the glass, Ma had prepared for the sorrow in life as well as the joy. She had been putting aside almost everything she earned sewing dresses at the shop for just such a catastrophe. And with the money, she taught Hyman a life lesson he was often to act on and never to forget. Help comes to those who help themselves.

"Now we will move to a place called Cleveland, near where your sister is living, and we will start a business there—maybe a grocery," said Hanna Golda. "You told me your sister has friends or cousins living nearby, didn't you, in a city called Detroit? We will be near them, near family."

. . .

With that, Pa embarked upon what seemed like a long life of following Ma, with her doing all the thinking for both of them. Ma was the brains of their business enterprise, and Hymie, as she called him, became the horse, doing all the heavy work. They moved to Cleveland and started a grocery store. Hymie actually got a horse and wagon, and he became the "fruit man," going in the mornings from street to street to sell produce from the store, thereby advertising its presence. Because of his easy open personality, and perhaps his strapping good looks, he was liked by everyone in the neighborhood. As he moved through the area called Huff on his wagon, people stopped him everywhere to chat, and inevitably wound up buying fruit from him and coming into the store in the afternoon to do their shopping.

"For a while I, how do you say it, 'choreographed' almost his every move," Ma explains. "I made him speak English in the house to me, even when we were alone, until he learned to speak it well. But I could never get him to read in English. He kept getting the letters mixed up with the Russian and the Hebrew letters he knew, and there were too many Yiddish newspapers around in Cleveland in that day for him to get any practice reading English. He would always come to me in the morning asking, 'How do I look?' and I would straighten the tie I made him wear when he was out in the wagon, or make him change his shirt because he had stained it while eating the night before. I told him to limit customers, before buying, to tasting only one of the many kinds fruits he carried on the wagon, so we wouldn't go broke feeding the neighborhood. I went to the central market with him, and to the bakery, to buy for the store. But the one thing I never had to do was teach him how to bargain the price down. Buying too much or too little, that was another thing. Hymie was no good at gaging how much of anything we needed. And, he never understood the concept of buying only what was selling in the store. 'Oh, look,' he would say, 'pineapples' but nobody bought them—'look *rogelachen,*' but our customers liked to make their own *rogelachen.*"

"He was well worth my efforts though. Your father was a loyal and a loving man. He would work twelve hours a day if I asked him to, cleaning the store, arranging the shelves, or whatever. And, he never complained about anything. He was very kind, and also a very strong man.

"We thrived in Cleveland, living in the upper half of a double on Eddy Rd. in the Glennville area, which was the heart of the Jewish community. There, we made numerous friends because I was social, and Hymie was an unobtrusive man, liked by many. We spent long hours together entertaining friends on the upper story front porch of our double, playing cards and talking of the past. He loved it, maybe because everybody was speaking Russian or Yiddish and drinking tea, and I never required him to speak English at those times unless somebody was speaking English to him."

Five years later, my brother Ben was is born. Pa idolized him. Ma raised him. Ben had a gift. He was to become a virtuoso at the violin and study at a place called "The settlement" in Cleveland. It was soon to become clear he had a future in music.

But before that, World War One came. During the "War

54

to End All Wars," according to Ma, not only did her father disappear, but the town that he lived in, "Stanislawow," also disappeared, or had its name changed. In fact, Galitzia itself disappeared, becoming a part of Russia at first, and then a part of Poland. The Russians invaded in 1914, only to be thrown out by a combined Austrian and German army the next year. Then the Austro-Hungarian Empire collapsed, leaving the Ukraine and the Poles locked into a mini-war over the city of Lvov. No more letters came from that part of the world for Ma. She read the newspapers avidly, but there was nothing in them about Stanislawow or Galitzia, except that it was now part of Poland.

When the war ended, word came that there was a pogrom in Poland. 150 residents were killed and hundreds were wounded. It didn't matter that Poland was a country with probably the largest or second largest population of Jews of any country in the world at the time. There was great animosity there against the Jewish population because the Jews had remained neutral in the fight between the Ukraine and Poland. The papers were filled with stories about President Wilson's appointment of a commission led by Henry Morgenthau, Sr. that was mandated to investigate the treatment of Jews in the newly established sovereign state of Poland.

Ma was convinced that somehow Rebbe Fogel had escaped to Palestine where he was safe, because she began receiving letters from two cousins, Libby and Rona, who were now living there, but she never received any proof that her father was there too. When she asked after him in her letters, nobody answered, except to say they knew nothing. Maybe he was living in Mei Sha'arim, the *Hassidic* section of Jerusalem, suggested Libby, but nobody knew because Mei Sha'arim was a place where secular females were not allowed, and Libby and Rona had not escaped from Europe only to become *chasids* in another country. They had escaped the strictures of ultra-orthodox Judaism in the

David Selcer

European pale, and become secular Jews who were not about
to go wandering through Mei Sha'arim, where they could get
stoned by the misogynous *Yeshiva Bauchers* (students of
Torah) who were living there.

Hymie was greatly worried about Ma's concerns for her
father because he knew Rebbe Fogel was the one Fogel with
whom she was close. Ma's mother had died when she was a
young girl and it had fallen completely to her father to raise
her. Aunts and cousins helped of course, however, basically,
Rebbe Fogel was the whole world for Hanna Golda as a
child.

Hymie also had his own worries. A year before World
War One ended, in March, 1917, the Czar abdicated, leaving
Russia with a provisional government. This was followed by
the "October Revolution," according to the Julian Calendar,
which Russia was still using. The October Revolution, also
known as The Bolshevik Revolution, actually occurred on
November 6-7, 1917, when the differences between the
Julian calendar and the Gregorian calendar, today's
internationally accepted civil calendar, are taken into
account. A horrendous civil war ensued between the
Bolsheviks, called the Reds, and the White Army, which was
a conglomeration of anti-communists, nationalists and highly
anti-Semitic conservative autocrats. The civil war lasted
until 1922. An ailing Vladimir Lenin, dictator of the new
Union of Soviet Socialist Republics, appointed Joseph Stalin
as the General Secretary of the Communist Party of the
Soviet Union's Central Committee. Stalin's brutality soon
began casting an ominous shadow over the Ukraine. Hyman
never heard from any of his immediate family back in Russia
again. Whether this was due to the Civil War between the
Reds and the Whites, the later Ukrainian famine forced farm
collectivization caused by Stalin's reign of terror, or the later
Nazi invasion, is unknown.

Except for his older sister, who emigrated to the United
States before him, and his youngest sister who married a man

from Bessarabia who brought her to the U.S. after Pa arrived, all that remains of his family are a few formal photographs of his mother and father taken by a professional photographer in Odessa around 1911 and a picture taken of his youngest sister somewhere in Bessarabia. There were also some second cousins with whom he had contact right after World War II, but the stories about that are very dim and untrustworthy.

SEVEN

"There are people who have never been taught anything, and know everything, have never been anywhere, and understand everything, have never given a moment's thought to anything, and comprehend everything. 'Blessed hands' is the name bestowed on these fortunate beings. The world envies, honors and respects them."

--Sholem Aleichem

While Ma and Pa are experiencing the ill effects of World War One, causing them great worries about their extended families back in Europe, my brother is growing up. He plays the violin. He is so good at it he is asked to join the Settlement, a special school for musicians in Cleveland from which many go on to the Julliard School of Music. "His talent is a blessing from on High," says Pa. "A person cannot just learn to play the violin like that on his own."

I follow Ben into the world in 1918. By age 12, I am playing the clarinet, but it soon becomes clear there is no future in music for me. Pa has everything to say about Ben's musical career and nothing to say about mine. Ben is talented. He is winning awards. "Look, he is being asked to solo at a public concert again," Pa says. Ben is winning this prize and that prize for his music. But Pa just doesn't seem to care what is happening in the music world with me.

"I can read music, just like Ben. I can play the clarinet and the oboe." I tell Pa. "I can follow the scores of whole symphonies as the orchestra plays them—just like a conductor. Why can't I go to the Settlement to study?"

Pa just clucks saying, "And when did they invite you to

come there?" You had to be invited to study at the
Settlement, and nobody had asked me. I don't know.
Maybe it had something to do with his command of the
English language, but Pa had a habit of being very direct,
almost brutal, and to the point, very untactful. He also had a
habit of belittling me. I took his words as an insult, yet I
don't know, maybe this was just his manner of speech,-- ie.
his way of saying that I had to be invited to go to the
settlement and if I wanted to go there I should do something
to see about getting them to invite me.

"I still don't understand it," I protested to my brother.
"Why were you invited to the Settlement to study, but not
me? I can play just as well as you, just on a different
instrument. I can play the clarinet and also the oboe."

"Yes, and technically you're very good, but you play
without any soul—without any heart. All you do is play, but
without any expression." I hate Ben when he tells me this.

Ben would have people he knew come over to the house
and play duets and quartets with him. Pretty girls, also
students at the Settlement, and even instructors from the
school, would come over to listen. One day Ben auditions to
become a player in the newly formed Cleveland Symphony
Orchestra. He is chosen--not to play the violin, but instead,
the viola. And, when he joins the orchestra, it seems like he
has joined a club full of avant guard enhusiastic people with
views and potential interests just like his. They would
discuss this guest conductor and this or that guest soloist,
often drinking beer, laughing and making fun of them, or
imitating how they played passages from rapturous
Hungarian dances or operatic overtures. They would go on
picnics together at Euclid Beach, and there put on free
concerts for the public. Our house seemed always filled with
music—not my music, but the music of the budding
Cleveland Symphony Orchestra.

I am just a tag-along. I have few friends, and they
seem to all want to play baseball and do other things at

which I am no good. But Ma says, "Don't worry. We will
send you to college. You'll have an education, maybe in
business. That's what you want anyway. Isn't it?" So Ben
goes off to the musician's world like a European, and I go
off to Ohio State University in Columbus, Ohio like an
American. There, I barely make it into the Ohio State
Concert Band, and I study accounting. I couldn't play in the
famed Ohio State Marching Band because I didn't play a
brass instrument, and I wasn't about to become a flugelhorn
player, which is what they needed, just so I could march with
them, although my desire to be in that band did kindle my
newly found interest in watching football.

Then, the black clouds move in. Ben falls in love with
Katie Rothman. The only problem is, Katie is Ben's first
cousin from Detroit, the city to where Pa's younger sister
Elizabeth had immigrated after Pa had been out of Russia for
almost five years. Pa's sister had married Bori Rothman
(actually Routmann) back in Bessarabia, and they both came
to the United States in 1910. A few years later Pa's sister
gives birth to Katie.

Ma absolutely prohibits Ben's relationship with Katie.
She does everything she can to break it up because the
bloodlines of Katie and Ben are too close. When Ma takes
action to break up the relationship, severe depression
envelops Ben. Ma enlists Katie's mother to prohibit Katie
from seeing him. When Katie rebuffs Ben, at her mother's
insistence, Ben can no longer get out of bed in the morning
and he doesn't want to eat. He can't bring himself to play the
viola anymore, and he misses too many practices with the
orchestra. Finally, he is asked to leave the symphony.

The whole matter precipitates unbearable emotional
controversy between Ben and Ma. He yells at her, driving
her to tears and he tells her he hates her. She urges him to
get over it, telling him that a boy shouldn't treat his mother
in this fashion, and invoking the fifth of the Ten
Commandments. But his response is to torment her by

refusing to come home at night, and telling her he has been up in Detroit with Katie.

Ben then became cruel to everyone in our family, including me. He treated Pa like an uneducated simpleton, showing him no respect. Finally, he just disappeared. He ran away. Ma calls everybody she can think of looking for Ben: Katie's mother; Ben's friends from the orchestra; his teachers at the Settlement; even the police. I was in college in Columbus at the time, which I thought to be a safe distance from all the drama gripping my family, but Pa insisted that I come home when Ben ran away. We had a huge argument over whether I would or not come home.

In one of the few times I ever saw my father exercise his authority as the man of the house, he insists that I suspend my college education and go find my brother to bring him back, because his absence is making my mother ill. "Why should I have to drop everything to go look for my brother," I demand? "I'm in the middle of my higher education! Doesn't that mean anything to you? I will miss the C.P.A. exam if I leave school now. Why should I have to do this?

"Because it is the right thing to do," Pa replies. "You will do it because you must do the right thing. It doesn't matter what you want to do. You will do it because it's right. Think of your brother. Think of your mother, not of yourself, and do what is right."

"Why don't you go look for him?"

"Because I have to stay here to help your mother with the store." Actually, I think it was because he didn't want to leave her while Ben was gone. She was so morose about his running away.

I never forgave either of them, Ben or my father, for this interruption of my life. I found Ben in Pittsburgh, where he had gone to look up one of his old girl friends who was studying music at the Carnegie Mellon School of Music. He was in a very bad way, seemingly unable to focus on any one subject long enough to express himself. His speech was

cluttered with a flight of ideas which he would continue to
express over and over again, not allowing anyone else to say
anything. He wanted to talk to anyone around as long, as he
could control the conversation, and his self-inhibition was
gone. He had no compunctions about exceeding the normal
barriers that would limit most people, suddenly believing
himself a great enough musical virtuoso to justify attempting
to buy himself a Stradivarius violin on which to practice. Of
course he couldn't afford it. But that wasn't going to stop
him. All this, and then: he'd break down crying, judging
himself to be of no worth, and he would fall into a funk
lacking any energy at all. It was during one of these lows
that I was able to get him on the train and home to
Cleveland. When we arrive, Ma calls the doctor.

As it turns out, it isn't actually the calamity of forbidden
love that is causing Ben's behavior. Ben is mentally ill,
according to the doctor, needing extensive therapy and,
perhaps, a new experimental procedure involving shock
treatments. Over time, we all began to realize that Ben is
sick, emotionally depressed, not necessarily because of
Katie, but because of something no doctor seemed to be able
to get his hands around. Pa remembered an uncle of his back
in Kherson who used to act a lot like Ben was acting,
creating controversy wherever he went and turning the
family's peace of mind into a shambles.

Ben becomes more and more cruel to my mother, and he
leaves home again and again. Each time it falls to me to find
him and to bring him back, "to do the right thing," if you
will, without any reward for myself. Eventually, he is
admitted off and on to the psychiatric unit at the Montefiore
Home in Cleveland, where he receives electro-shock
treatments. Pa, who seems to be away more than he is home
now for long stints of time, never says anything about this,
except that he expects me to go out and find Ben when he
runs away. Each time, Pa forgives Ben for causing upheaval,
and he tries to calm Ma down. As for me, I never receive so

much as a thank you. Running after Ben is just expected of me.

All I really wanted, if I couldn't be a professional musician like my brother, was to be a CPA—a businessman, not a bookkeeper or even just an accountant. But that was never to be. What I wanted for myself didn't seem to matter to Pa, and my mother was too overcome with catering to my brother, the great musician, to talk about it. Ma and Pa spend all their time trying to get Ben better so he can go back to playing with the Cleveland Symphony. They don't have any time for me.

So, instead, I put distance between my family and myself, and I try to forget about my own desires. I become absorbed with my girlfriend, Sonia, who later becomes my wife. I spend great amounts of time with Sonia's family, her sister, Marion, and her brother, Leo, as well as with her mother and father, and I just grow further and further away from my own family. Sonia's brother, Leo, and sister, Marion, really seem to care about me, and we become fast friends.

Leo is quite the musician in his own right, playing the oboe, though not professionally. Sonia's sister is married to a real businessman, Ben Goldman, who runs a mattress factory, a real mover and shaker—somebody to look up to. He provided a home not only for his wife and their three children, but also for his wife's parents, upon whom the depression had come down very hard. They live in the same large house with them --ie. my girlfriend's mother and father. They lost their candy store business in the years immediately following 1929, and Sonia's father now makes a living pursuing his old trade, which is that of tailor. He conducts his tailor's business out of the large house Ben Goldman provides for them all in Cleveland Heights.

So Ben Goldman is not only an attractive "with it guy," but also a saving angel for my girlfriend's entire family. At least until one day four men knock at the front door asking for Ben Goldman. They claim they run an olive oil business down in the part of town called "Little Italy," and that there is something Mr. Goldman has to do if he doesn't want to wind up with his legs broken. As it turns out, Ben Goldman had been gambling regularly, playing cards and shooting craps, at a bookie-joint on the near West Side, and he owes a lot of money that he can't pay. The mob has come to collect. Sonia's mother just can't abide it. She thinks the mob men are *gonifs* (thieves) and that Ben is a lawbreaker. She hates all things illegal. I can still hear her yelling about it. Here is where I learn my first really big lesson of life. *Not all is as it seems.*

"Don't worry," Ben Goldman says. "My brothers will loan me the money."

He had four brothers in Chicago, all of whom were also in the mattress business. But his collective solicitation of help from them results in a unified "No" from the Goldman brothers.

Sonia's mother goes berserk when she hears this, and she throws Ben Goldman, her own son-in-law, out of the house—*his own house*—*confirmation for me that not all people in life are as good as they seem.* He and his wife Marion never see each other again but they also never divorce. Instead he sends money to her religiously to keep up the house for her three children, her parents and her. But he is always *persona non-gratis* thereafter, and no-one in the household ever mentions him again.

Then, World War II comes to the United States. My brother is now safely back playing with the Cleveland Orchestra, and in any event also safe from the draft because of his previous medical history, and probably his age. But I am a prime candidate for the military service. I was drafted in 1942 and spent two years in the army.

Not only had my college career been interrupted by my brother's precipitous wonderings, and not only had my earlier hopes for a career in music been blocked by circumstance, but now it seemed that history itself was going to frustrate me from getting my first job after college. Instead I would be going into the army.

So I got married to my girlfriend and went off to the army for two years. Again Sonia's mother goes berserk, because we ran away and got married by a justice of the peace in Kentucky. To her, we weren't really married, and we were living in sin. She insists that we have a full blown Jewish wedding in the synagogue, which we did when I was in Cleveland on leave during the next Thanksgiving holiday.

But all of these crazies—Ben Goldman's gambling career; my shotgun synagogue wedding; and my brother's shock treatments—pale in comparison to what happened when I came home after the war. A few months after the war Pa just upped and disappeared. Hyman Zeltzer had just gone away, creating a hiatus during which I never really knew where he was or what he was doing. He did not come back for almost a year and a half.

As far as I was concerned, the man was not a very good father to me. He'd insisted that I interrupt college on more than one occasion to go find Ben. He had expressed no understanding of my own desires, and he was more concerned about my brother Ben than about me.

So it was time for me to be more concerned with my own life than about where Pa was or what he was doing. Out of a feeling of obligation, I probed my mother about where he'd gone and what he was doing, but she seemed very reluctant to answer, as if it was her business and nobody else's. *Fine*, I thought. I really didn't care that much.

EIGHT

"A kind word is no substitute for a piece of herring or a bag of oats"

-- Sholem Aleichem

"Now, sitting *shiva* for Pa, there was little else to do but remember all of the things I could remember about him, and these things, haunted me with questions. Where was Pa between the end of World War II and the beginning of 1948? He just seemed to disappear right after I got out of the military service, and then he re-appeared only twice, both times during periods when my brother was getting sick again. Why did he show so much compassion for Ben, yet continue to treat me without understanding or kindness? And, what had happened to his dedication to Ma?

When pressed about these things before he died, all Ma would say was, "I know he loves you more than you know." As for his absence, she would say vaguely that Pa was away helping his relatives when he was gone—but where? What relatives? And why was I finding envelopes addressed to her around the house when I would visit that had stamps on them from Portugal, Spain, Italy and Cyprus? Of course the letters these envelopes contained were all in Yiddish, so I couldn't read or understand them.

It was really kind of sad. When my own sons were four and one years old, nobody would really say where their grandfather had been during late 1946 and 1947. Every inquiry met with vague explanations or, worse yet, deflection of the questions.

Nonetheless, almost thirty years later, on the day after

the funeral, I decided at Pa's *shiva* to pursue the matter again. "Ma," I asked, the day after the funeral. "You remember when Pa was away all that time after World War II ended, and you said he was away doing things for his cousins and uncles? Where was he? What was he doing? And, why did we have him buried in Israel? The only mention the rabbi made about Pa's place of interment was when he announced where the burial would take place--Israel. 'Hyman Zeltzer gave a lot to Israel,' the rabbi said. I didn't even know Pa had anything to give to Israel, or to anyone else. He left no will, and to my knowledge, no estate."

My questions about where he'd been during those lost two years after the war seemed to irritate Ma. "Why are you asking me this now—at the time of his funeral?"

And she seemed downright aggravated by my questions about Israel and his burial there. "You never wanted to know about your father before. Frankly, I don't feel like talking about it at this time. It was the only big argument Hymie and I ever had. He left me alone during this time, and I can't bear to talk about it right now. Not now."

"But Ma, Why Israel—"

"If you want to know anything, you'll have to ask Mr. Bloom."

"Does Ben know about it?"

"No, you'll have to ask Mr. Bloom."

. . .

Herschel and Yetta Bloom were the dearest friends of my parents. She passed away two years ago, but he was still very much alive. They had lived together on a farm out near Mentor, Ohio, near the lake—Lake Erie that is. So far as I knew, Herschel still lived there. When I was a child, my family and the Blooms spent many happy days at that farm, picking apples from Herschel's orchard. Ma and Yetta would then spend weekends making apple sauce.

Herschel did not come to the funeral because he was too old and ill to make the trip from Mentor to attend. He had been hard of hearing, almost deaf, from the time I first knew him, and he didn't like to talk on the phone. Why was my mother going to make me take the time to drive out to Mentor if I wanted to know more about Pa's life between 1945 and 1948? Was it some sort of punishment for my earlier lack of interest in him? All I really knew about Herschel and my Pa was that the two of them were very close, especially in their older age, like pals, almost like war buddies.

On the few occasions my new wife and I visited the Bloom farm after World War II, I noticed Herschel and Pa, then in their late 60s, spending hours together drinking tea and vodka, and laughing about things they remembered and places they'd been. They always spoke of these things in Yiddish, which I did not understand very well at all. They were too old to serve in the military during World War II, and I knew Pa had not been involved in World War One, but somehow it seemed like they'd shared experiences in a war together, just not a war that anyone remembered as being part of World War I or a part of World War II. They spoke about a place called Athlit, of which I'd never heard, and about places called Xlotympou and Caraolos on the Island of Cyprus. They talked of deals with people in Czechoslovakia. They discussed something called *Ma'abarot*, about which I knew nothing and had no curiosity.

Back then, I had a starter-family, a boy who was six and another one who was two, and it always seemed to me that Pa should have been spending his time playing with them when we were at the farm, not jawing over old times with Mr. Bloom. Hymie, my mother would say to him in Yiddish, "Stop already with all the *alt geshikhtem* (old stories), and take your *einiclach* (grandchildren) down to the orchard. Better you should be picking an *epl* (apple)." And

that would do it. Pa always did what she wanted, when she
wanted it done, both before he went away, and after he came
back to stay. So Pa and Herschel would end their
conversations, and the *alt geshikhtem* would end. What did
it matter to me? I couldn't understand them anyway. They
were speaking in Yiddish.

But why was Ma now making me go to Mr. Bloom to
find out what was going on with Pa during the time he was
gone from our family? Were Ma and Pa estranged during
that period of time? Had my father done something wrong?
Was he on the run from somebody? Maybe it was that my
brother Ben had gotten to be too much for him and he just
had to get away. I just didn't know. And, why was Ma so
reluctant to talk about it now?

She seemed angry that in the intervening years I'd never
asked Pa to tell me the *alt geshikhtem* in English that he and
Mr. Bloom used to speak about in Yiddish. Was she angry
that I'd never examined her about this before, always
accepting her most cursory of answers? "Oh, he's away
helping his relatives." But helping them to do what?
Certainly she knew where Pa was and what he was doing
during those times, but she was not about to discuss it.

And, I certainly wasn't going to drop everything and
drive out to the Bloom farm now, just to have an old man
explain the *alt geshikhtem* to me in English. I knew,
however, that Mr. Bloom was getting to be a very old man,
and that if Ma continued her reticence on the matter of Pa's
absence, the relevance, if any, of the old stories to that period
would be lost forever. Then, probably nobody would ever
know where Hyman Zeltzer went or what he did during this
period, which I had always thought of as "The Great Hiatus."
Oh well, if that was what was to be, so be it! I was not going
to worry about it.

• • •

Two weeks later, however, I found myself still obsessed with my almost total lack of any previous knowledge about my father, who he was, or what he'd done in life. I kept reflecting on what happened after he came home to stay. But by then, I hardly ever saw him. Two years after "The Great Hiatus," as I referred to the time he was away from Ma, he and Ma moved to Miami, Florida, Coral Gables to be exact. It was 1950. From then until they moved back to Cleveland in 1970, I only saw them once a year for about three weeks to a month, when they came north to visit my family and Ben's family in the summer time, or for special occasions like Bar Mitzvah's, weddings and their fiftieth wedding anniversary. They'd spend three weeks with my family in July and three weeks with Ben's family in August. These were the hottest months in Miami.

Ben still lived in Cleveland, but we'd moved to a small town about an hour south of Cleveland so I could take my first real job. I'd finally made it through college after the multiple interruptions my brother had caused in my education, and I'd completed my time in the army. Ma and Pa got me a job through some wealthy friends of theirs they called the Weitzmans, who, among other things, ran a small distillery outside a little Ohio town. The only stipulation was that I had to begin working immediately because I was needed to replace someone who'd just died. I was to be the accountant for the distillery. As I now had a wife and two children, I considered this a godsend, but I never followed the normal progression to my education by taking the CPA exam. Circumstances did not permit it. I was to be an accountant, but not a Certified Public Accountant, and that saddened me.

"What difference does it make," asked Pa during one of the few times he was home right after the war? "We got you a job. You're working. You're putting food on the table for your family. What else could you want?" True to form, Pa was continuing to watch me perform, as I had on my clarinet, without ever tossing a kind word my way.

Cedar Valley Distillery where I worked, was in Wooster, Ohio. Wooster had sixty Jewish families and it was very nice for us. There were some couples our age there, all with children, and my wife and I were friendly with all of them. Actually, age didn't really matter. The older Jewish families in town all took an interest in any new family that moved to the area. So we knew all of them too. A low interest loan under the Servicmen's Readjustment Act of 1944, known as the GI Bill, enabled me to get a mortgage and buy one of the "cracker-box" houses being built on the edge of town. There, we lived in the same neighborhood as our friends. The only thing really missing from my life was an automobile. We didn't have a car. I walked two and a half miles to work and back each day. But that problem was soon to be solved by a precipitous opening in the events that had shackled my life up until then.

A family that had owned the department store in town since the Civil War, the Friedingers, decided to make a gift to the local Jewish community of enough money to finance the building of a small synagogue. Previously, we had been using a rented frame house on McKinley Avenue as our meeting house, qua synagogue. It was ramshackle, and we sat on card-table chairs that scraped across the wooden floors in the living-dining area whenever services were conducted, which wasn't very often. We had only one real Torah, which was kept in an antique cabinet, with removed doors and a blue curtain with an embossed Star of David across the opening. It served as our holy ark. The Freidingers announced they would give their gift to the community with only one stipulation: that every family commit to a pledge, payable over time, of at least $1000.00 toward the new building.

"I won't do it," I told my wife.

"You will do it," she retorted. "It is necessary to

71

maintain our status in the community."

"Status? Status be damned. I can't afford it. I haven't got the money."

"Then do what Sammy suggested," she replied. "Borrow it. For once in your life, take a risk." Sammy Gordon was one of our friends. He was in business with his father, and he had a modicum of wealth.

"How would I ever pay it back," I asked?

"I don't know. Talk to Sammy about that."

So one Saturday over breakfast at Kienie's Cafeteria, I broached my dilemma with Sammy. I told him that I couldn't even afford a car on what I made, but here were the Freidingers asking me for a one-thousand-dollar pledge toward the new synagogue. I didn't have that kind of money. I didn't make that kind of money at the distillery, and if I borrowed it I was afraid I would not be able to pay it back. Sammy's reply startled me.

"Don't borrow $1000. Borrow $2000, and pay half of it toward the new synagogue. The other half you should invest with me. I'm buying a business in Akron,-- you know, Akron, Ohio. It's a steel fabrication and erection business. I no longer want to work for my father, running his junk yard. I can do better. Besides, I can run the junk yard while I'm doing more up in Akron, with your help. You'll do the books and you'll manage the place when I'm not there—like a partner. I'll give you a 10% interest for your investment with me and pay you a decent salary. I'll also solve your transportation problem so you can get back and forth from Akron to your home here." There's only one condition. If the business really gets going, you must move to Akron where you can keep an eye on it day and night.

"For once in your life take a risk," said my wife. "You hate working at the distillery. You hate it that your parents got that job for you. You hate it that you don't have a car. You're a frustrated musician who'll never get a break in the music world like your brother. And it's too late now for you

to study and pass the CPA test, having been away from
school for five years and now having two kids and a wife to
support. Admit it, you'll never be a CPA So take a risk.
Go out on your own. Become a businessman and stop
blaming your father and your brother for what you think are
the failings in your life. It's either that, or I'm going out to
get a job. How would you like that?" It was the early fifties,
and then if a married woman worked to help support her
family, it said something about the man.

Stunned by her response, I went to work for my friend
Sammy who was setting up a new business in Akron. How
could I refuse? Finally, I was becoming a businessman. My
title was to be Comptroller, and I was to own 10% of the
business. Now all we had to do was make the business
work.

By this time Ma and Pa had moved away from
Cleveland to Miami, Florida, but annually they came up
north to spend three weeks with Ben's family and three with
mine. When they got to our house that year, I asked if I
could borrow the money from them that I needed to pay for
my share of the business. The answer I got was almost
predictable.

"Lester," Pa said, "if we had that kind of money to loan
you for something like this we would, but we don't. I wish it
were otherwise." Then came the unpredictable part of the
answer. "But we see your house needs a painting, so your
mother and I are going to paint it for you, and we'll buy the
paint We'll start tomorrow."

Just what I didn't want or need—my two elderly parents
clamoring over the outside of my house on ladders, painting
it. I couldn't understand why they didn't have the money to
spare. They'd come up with what they needed to move to
Florida and to buy a house there from the sale of their
grocery store in Cleveland. They'd also come up with the
money to pay for all Ben's hospital stays. Why now did they
suddenly not have any money?

So I borrowed the thousand dollars from the bank that I needed to go into business with Sammy. The other thousand dollars I also borrowed, and I gave it to the Friedinger Campaign for the new synagogue. That enabled me to become a businessman and saved our name in town, but believe me, there were plenty of times I wished I'd have kept that other thousand and put it into the business when we needed it. Ultimately, however, things started to go well in Akron, and it became time for me to move my family there.

And, that's when Pa shocked my socks off. Without my asking, he offered to *give* me two thousand dollars to help us buy the house we needed in Akron. I was dying to ask him how he'd suddenly come up with the money, and why, but my wife told me not to do it. I simply did not understand the man, but I graciously thanked him.

NINE

"If you listen carefully, you get to hear everything you didn't want to hear in the first place."
                                               -- Sholem Aleichem

For the next 25 years, or so, I wondered why Pa had conducted himself in this manner—at first refusing to loan me the money I wanted, and then later just giving me more than the amount for which I had originally asked. Perhaps, that is why, two weeks after Pa's funeral, my brother Ben and I had a conversation about this. Somehow it felt to me like I hadn't even been in the family, that I really hadn't understood what was really going on. I was missing something and I didn't know what it was. Pa was always so solicitous and accommodating of Ben, especially when it came to his career, yet when it came to me, he was harsh and demanding, never afraid to pass his judgment.

"You will do it because it's the right thing to do," he would say. "How can you leave your mother and me alone with this circumstance?" There was always guilt on my part when it came to me. I was always treated as if I didn't know right from wrong, or that I was asking for too much. Somehow, I was made to feel that I didn't deserve anything.

Although we were by no means close to each other, I determined to discuss my perception of the position I held in the family from Pa's point of view, with my older brother Ben. That was not an easy thing for me to do although I wanted to learn his perspective.

There were many things Ben had done that I felt were wrong, and I looked upon him as often being completely

75

impractical and completely lacking in common sense, but I also looked up to him because of his talent, and well, probably just because he was my older brother. When I asked him why he thought I'd received the treatment I'd received from Pa, before he answered, he required me to give him a long explication of exactly what I thought that treatment was. I found this to be very painful.

"Perhaps it was because you were the younger brother," Ben said.

I laughed. "That simple--Huh?"

"No I'm quite serious." Ben continued, using his intellectual tone. "There were only two boys in Pa's family you know. All of the rest of his siblings were girls, and of the two boys, Pa was the younger brother. Do you know anything about his older brother? His name was Shmuel."

"No, until the funeral I didn't even know he had an older brother."

"Well, I did," Ben responded. "You probably didn't know anything about Pa's older brother because he never made it to this country, but Ma told me he was a prodigy back in Russia. Without a doubt he had the reputation of being the finest *khazn* (cantor) alive at the time in Kherson. In fact, the man's voice was acclaimed all over the Ukraine. He was a tenor. He was musical. They said he sang with such a lyrical voice that it could tear your heart out. On the High Holidays people would flock to the Great Choral Synagogue of Kherson to hear Shmuel Zelitzer's rendition of the most important prayer of the New Year—*Kol Nidre* Of course, she got all this from talking to Pa.

"You know Pa's father was orthodox, like every other Jew in Kherson at the time, but not what we would call ultra-orthodox today. Yet he took great pride in his eldest son's study of Torah and his religious observance. Pa, on the other hand was not the best student at *cheder.* Nor was he in the least bit observant.

"Shmuel even gave Pa's father some prominence in the community. When he walked into the Temple, everyone knew he was the father of the *Great Khazn of Kherson*, (Cantor of Kherson) and they would nod to him. Music was always a big thing in their household. Once the crown prince of Kherson Oblast even visited the synagogue just so Shmuel could put on a concert for him. And there were invitations from Kiev for him to sing at the Ukrainian National Opera House."

"So it sounds like musical talent was not just an accident in our family. We have a tradition of it," I said.

"That is correct."

"And it was a tradition that Pa saw you as carrying on Ben," I added.

"Maybe," Ben mused. "But I certainly didn't carry on the religious tradition, only the musical tradition. I do know," he continued, "that Shmuel could read music like me, and that Pa's family sent him for voice training when they realized how good a singer he was, which is the same thing that happened to me with my violin training a generation later, but it was training with my fiddle. Music was definitely one of the family traditions."

"But Pa didn't see me as carrying on that tradition, did he?" I groused

"No. Just as he was, you were the younger brother. It was amazing how a Russian family that was by no means wealthy could come up with the money for voice lessons for Shmuel. Pa, on the other hand was left to apprentice as a machinist with his uncle."

"Are you saying that because of Pa's position as the younger brother, he became accustomed to not receiving the same attention his older brother received. So he felt that, I, as the younger brother, didn't deserve the things you got as the older brother. Is that what you're saying?"

No. I'm not trying to say that."

"Then what are you saying?"

"I think what I'm saying is, that just as Pa had to find his own way in the world without having a professional career to rely on, he may have felt you also should have to find your own way. He may have thought it would make you stronger."

"But this is all just speculation on your part, isn't it Ben," I complained. "You don't really know what was in his mind do you. You're just giving me this history lesson and speculating about its meaning because you never really saw me do anything wrong that would warrant the treatment I got from Pa."

"No. I never saw you do anything really wrong, but here's something else you wouldn't have known about Pa's brother Shmuel.

"What was that?"

"That Shmuel was a very weak person, physically and mentally. He was a twin, and his twin brother died in an accident when he was ten years old, for which Shmuel blamed his father. Out in the stable, his twin got too close to the wrong end of a horse and he was kicked and trampled to death as the horse backed over him. Shmuel, who witnessed the whole incident was deeply affected. He blamed his father for putting the horse in its stall without tethering it, which allowed the horse to back up. From that day forward, he would never ride or drive a horse because he was terrified of them. He had to be driven everywhere he went by somebody else. He was also deeply affected emotionally by this event, often breaking down in crying fits for what seemed to others to be no reason at all. This always happened on his birthdays and around holidays that involved memorial services for the dead. Nobody could speak of his twin brother without encouraging Shmuel's wrath to the point of tears.

"Pa once told Ma that it put a tremendous strain on his family, to the point where people just stopped talking about Shmuel's dead twin brother altogether. Pa's father never

spoke of Shmuel's twin brother to Shmuel again. Nobody
did. Nobody could."

"So what finally happened to Shmuel? They never sent
him to the United States. Why not? They sent Pa's older
sister instead, and after Pa got here, they sent his younger
sister.

Why did they not send Shmuel?"

"Because around 1910 or 1911, he ran away from home,
and nobody ever heard from him again."

I was dumbfounded. Pa's older brother had run away
from home, just like Ben had run away from home. The
only difference was that I brought Ben back. There was a
long silence between us as Ben cast his eyes downward.
Was he drawing an analogy to himself? If so, not only was it
the first time I'd ever heard him referring, at least
symbolically, to his own condition, but it was astounding
that he also seemed to be characterizing it as a mental or
emotional weakness. Nobody had ever talked about this in
our family before. Pa avoided it. Ma avoided it and I just
avoided it too.

Why was he telling me about Shmuel's running away
now, all of a sudden, while I was in the process of trying to
pin him down on what made Pa act the way he did toward
me? Was Ben possibly trying to say that it was his fault
that Pa treated me the way he did? Was he saying that just
like in Pa's immediate family with Shmuel, my own Ma and
Pa gave all their attention to Ben because he was the one
who needed it the most?

That might answer some of the questions I had, but not
all of them. It didn't answer the question of why I was not
encouraged in my own music career. It didn't answer the
question of why I always seemed to get the harsh end of the
stick when there was really no reason for it. It didn't explain
things like why Pa refused me a loan when I asked him for it
so I could go into business with Sammy Gordon in Akron,
and then turned around and voluntarily actually *made a gift*

to me of twice as much money as I'd asked to borrow. The gift was to help me buy a house in Akron when Sammy and I had finally gotten the business going on our own. Why did he first withhold his financial help, and then turn around and make a gift to me? There were other inconsistencies too. For instance, why, when I was young, was our house always open to Ben's friends, but seemingly not to mine? When I wanted to have Sonia's family over, Pa said, "No, that would be inappropriate," but then he changed his mind, telling me that she and her brother and sister could come over but not her parents. All my life, I lived feeling that there was something wrong in our family, something that other families did not have to suffer. Finally, I just confronted Ben straight away about this.

"Ben, if there was something wrong, I did that made Pa be so rigid with me and inconsiderate of my feelings, just tell me what it was. Will you? There's nothing more horrible than when everybody around you knows there's something wrong, but nobody will tell you what it is."

"No, no I never noticed him being like that to you, and I also never thought you'd done anything wrong," Ben replied. He was skirting the subject, avoiding the question, maybe just to be diplomatic.

There was more I wanted to know, and it didn't sound like Ben was going to be able to help me. "So tell me Ben," I continued. "Do you know where Pa went when he literally disappeared for two years after World War II ended?"

"That's something about which I can be of no help to you I'm afraid," he said.

"Well did he just go away? Was he just another Zeltzer runaway," I asked facetiously?

"No need for an attitude like that on the subject we're discussing here," Ben retorted. Shmuel had his reasons for running away, and when I left home, I certainly had important reasons for leaving too—at least important to me. I have no idea if Pa was running away, but I doubt it. When he left home I don't know where he went during that time period, or what he did. If he was running from something, I have no idea what it was. All I know is that by then I had married, and I was having some pretty difficult times of my own. I wasn't looking after Pa because I had no time for that. But you should have more respect for your father than to say a thing like that. What do you think, that our family has some sort of trait involving running away from things?"

"Well. What about Ma? Didn't you care at all what effect Pa's absence was having on her?" Ben just looked away. "Didn't you even ask her where he'd gone? I know I certainly did."

I knew the answer before I'd even finished asking the question. No. Ben hadn't even cared enough to ask where Pa was. Instead, he'd gotten sick again, and when that happened, his sickness was all-consuming. Strange, how nobody outside our immediate family ever knew that Ben was sick, other than his wife and his doctor. I guess it was just a time when people didn't reveal what was going on behind their own curtains to other people, and nobody looked to see for themselves. But I certainly knew what was going on, and I'm sure Pa did too, because he would come home for short periods of time when Ben was sick. I had just gotten out of the army, and my attention was completely focused on setting up a new household in Wooster at the time with Sonia. Ma was lonely and stuck with caring for Ben. Everybody had their problems, but Ben didn't care. He was too self-consumed.

For some reason I felt that this period of Pa's absence I knew nothing about, because of Ma's reluctance to talk about it, and Ben's inability to do so, held the secrets I needed to know about Pa in order to understand him. I was thrown off balance by the stories I'd heard, but never known before, about him at the funeral, and I was despairing because it seemed like I had missed everything that was good and interesting about him. The gap in my knowledge about my own father's whereabouts between 1946 and 1948 was beginning to obsess me, and it was apparent that the only source I had left to fill it was going to have to be Herschel Bloom.

"Well, you've convinced me," I told Ben. "There wasn't any conspiracy in the family to keep the truth from me about my own position in it, even though at one time I thought there might have been, with you Ma and Pa on one side, and me alone on the other. What's become clear from this conversation is that, except for a few stories from the old country, you know almost as little about Pa as I do." I was lying. Ben's conversation had actually given me insight into a lot of the things that may have motivated Pa's actions toward me. Nonetheless, I kept up my deception that Ben's comments had been unhelpful.

"Ma told me that if I want to know what Pa was doing during the two years after the war, I should ask Herschel Bloom, not her. It's become clear to me," I grouse, "that even though I don't want to go out to Mentor to ask Mr. Bloom my questions about this, I'm going to have to do that."

"Well, you better get out there right away before he dies," Ben remarked. I couldn't tell whether this remark was tongue-in-cheek or not, but I went, sooner rather than later. One morning I drove, alone, from Akron to Cleveland and then out to Mentor to see Bloom.

TEN

"Life is a dream for the wise, a game for the fool, a comedy for the rich, a tragedy for the poor."

-- **Sholem Aleichem**

It's not easy to picture a person from Transylvania, the ancestral home of Dracula, as an Ohio farmer. But that's what Herschel Bloom is, a Hungarian--or was Transylvania a part of Romania when he left? Here's what I know about Heschel Bloom, as related to me over the years by my mother, and from a little historical research I've done on the side.

Herschel was born near the town of Brasov in the Carpathian Mountains. His family soon moved to the city of Oradea in eastern Hungary, where they greatly benefitted from the liberalizing revolution of 1848 sweeping Western Europe and allowing Jews to rise to middle and upper middle class status. Jewish Emancipation occurred in the latter half of the 19th Century in the Austro-Hungarian Empire, permitting them the right to vote and to live anywhere they wished in Oradea. It started with the principles and wars of the of the French Revolution and ended with the resolutions and tactics of the Congress of Berlin, where among many other things, the granting of equal rights to Jews in most of Europe was raised. In the intervening 90 years, Jewish emancipation became a political and legal fact in all European countries where revolution and liberalism were in ascendency: France, Belgium, the Netherlands, Italy, Germany, and Austria-Hungary.

Headed for the comfort of a banker's career at the dawn

of the 20th Century, Herschel leads a charmed life, with a huge extended family surrounding him, numbering among its members a doctor, a lawyer, two professors and the owners of a large family carriage manufacturing business. Growing up in a big baroque style home in the Olosig neighborhood of Oradea near the river, his family becomes so assimilated that they attend a synagogue where the sermons are delivered in Hungarian rather than Yiddish. But the outbreak of World War One ruins it all. Herschel is 24 at the time.

Almost three years into the war, the declining Habsburg Austro-Hungarian Empire begins splitting up, with Hungary, the weaker of its two parts, swinging toward socialism and then toward soviet style communism, and Austria leaning toward a conservative German/Prussian version of universal manhood suffrage. The conservative Prussians hate the communists. Many of the Hungarian socialists are Jews, and so as communism begins taking hold in Transylvania, virulent anti-Semitism rises again in the form of something called the "White Terror."

Fearing the mayhem of these oncoming massive changes, Herschel and his parents leave Hungary for the United States, deserting the rest of the family which prefers to stay in Europe, trying to cope with the fall-out from the world war. Arriving in America with their old country wealth still in-tact, Herschel's immediate family spends judiciously, lives moderately, and then they "short-sell" a number of high flying stocks in the summer of 1929 preceding the American stock market crash. The short-selling yields great profits, enough to purchase many acres of land near Lake Erie's shore, about twenty-five miles east of Cleveland, which Herschel's father hopes to cultivate into a vineyard for a family wine business. All of this occurs during the Great Depression that followed the crash of 1929. Land is very cheap now, and Herschel's father believes that owning it, as was the case back in Europe, is the key to sustained wealth.

The family's contemplated grape enterprise, however, soon changes from wine production into the production of cider and other apple products because the real estate they have purchased is covered with dilapidated apple orchards that can be restored more inexpensively than they can be dug up for the installation of new grape vineyards. The Blooms also decide to keep a substantial portion of their land in potato production for conversion into gin and vodka in the Canadian distilleries across the lake and to the north in Montreal. Their Canadian contact, Samuel Bronfman, turns their commerce with him into a profitable source of revenue over the next few years because it's legal to distill whiskey in Canada but not in the United States. The cheap Canadian whiskey can be illegally run across the border by the mob and sold in the northern U.S. cities of Boston, New York and Chicago during the prohibition era.

So the American Bloom's flourish, but letters from their extended family across the Atlantic tell of ill fortune and financial collapse for their uncles, aunts and cousins in Transylvania. Hungary lies bleeding on its back from World War I. Even before a peace treaty is concluded, communists and non-communists struggle with each other to set up new governments in Hungary and in Romania, which leads to two slaughters, the first called the Red Terror against conservatives and monarchists, and the second called the White Terror, a reaction against the communists. The White terrorists ultimately prevail, but not before virulent anti-Semitism reappears, resulting in 3000 deaths during the White Terror because so many Jews are communists and liberals. In the meantime, the Romanians invade and snatch Transylvania from Hungary. Cries for advice, help with immigration and financial assistance then begin persisting in the correspondence from the now impoverished European Blooms across the ocean to the American Bloom family.

Meanwhile, Herschel, an only child, becomes the sole beneficiary of his family's American fortune, but upon inheriting the farm he realizes he has little interest in agriculture. Social justice issues and work associated with the public good excite him more, as does his unrelenting concern for his relatives in Europe. As his wife describes it, Herschel inherited the "professionalism gene" from the European Blooms and all the dreams that come with it, and he wants to use it to do something *pro bono* for them. But what?

In 1930, after the deaths of his parents, two pamphlets arrive in the mail with Canadian postage on them: one from the Canadian Jewish Congress (CJC) Committee for Refugees; and the other from the United Jewish Relief Agencies (UJRA), both embossed with the notice "FUNDS NEEDED FOR TRAPPED JEWISH REFUGEES IN EUROPE, and both with warm handwritten personal notes stating,

"Herschel,

In memory of your dear parents whom I knew well and loved, I hope you will see fit to contribute to this worthwhile cause. Who among us does not have relatives in Europe in need of what-ever support we can give them?

Warmly,
Sam Bronfman"

The pamphlets contain a legend at the bottom stating: "A fund established by the Zionist Organization of North America. Bring the Jews of Europe to a national home in Palestine."

Samuel Bronfman chairs both organizations. Upon reading the pamphlets, Herschel realizes he now has a *pro bono* cause to which he can devote himself.

He contributes significant amounts to both charities

immediately. He also goes to Canada the next year to attend the general assembly of the Canadian Jewish Congress, where he hopes to meet Samuel Bronfman personally. There he learns of the Ha'Apala Program, which is preparing for the migration of European Jews to Palestine. At the time, immigration of European Jews into North America in significant numbers is curtailed by the policies of the United States and Canada. Great Britain's Balfour Declaration, however, is supporting the establishment of a "National Home for the Jewish People" in Palestine. Imbued with the hope this inspires for the Jews of Europe who are quickly becoming outliers, Herschel takes up the cause of a Zionism.

In the meantime, he and his wife Yetta become fast friends with my mother and father, Anne and Hyman Zeltzer, largely as a result of their doing business with each other in the farmer's market in Cleveland. Hyman often speaks to Herschel of his rising dismay over the loss of contact with his brother and sisters back in Russia and Anne's loss of contact with her father. When Herschel comes back from the CJC general assembly in Canada, he's full of information and exuberance about what could be done through Jewish organizations to help the situations of both their families back in Europe.

"But we have no money to contribute to these groups," Hyman protests"

"Then contribute your time," Herschel answers. "You can contribute your time. Money is not the only answer. The CJC and the UJRA will be making arrangements to buy ships for the transport of Jewish refugees to Palestine. People are needed to help with these plans."

"But who would want to live in Palestine," Hyman asks? "To give up a life in Europe to live somewhere in the desert is ridiculous. Better they should come here."

"Living here in America it's easy to think that way," Herschel persists, "but how would you like to live in a country where you didn't have the right to vote; in a country where the tax collector just came and took your money without you having any say; or where everybody around you considered you to be a second class citizen, or not even a citizen at all? That is what being a Jew in Eastern Europe is getting to be like again today. Your civil rights are becoming fewer and fewer; your political rights are non-existent; and, your economic rights are boxed in by outdated rules and social conventions. And, the United States won't let you in because of its immigration quotas."

"I don't think Hymie understands what you're saying," Anne interrupts.

"Then explain it to him in words he can understand." Herschel says impatiently.

The Yiddish conversation that ensues between Hyman and Anne is loud and long-winded, basically covering subjects like pogroms and poverty, exclusions from jobs and losses of money; and the indifference of police to the rights of Jews. Hyman keeps insisting that the things Herschel is talking about are the same pie-in-the-sky things his Uncle Meyer kept bending his ears about as a boy—Zionism, Palestine, political rights, having your own army and your own police. He couldn't see the relevance of any of them back in Russia as he travelled about listening to his Uncle Meyer's views.

"It didn't make sense to me then, and it doesn't make sense to me now," he argues. "I say let us keep our money and not give it away for this."

And that's how it came to be that Herschel and Yetta were Zionists, but Anne and Hymie were not. Yet they were still friends, very close friends. Anne and Yetta would spend long hours on the Blooms' farm making apple sauce together, and Herschel and Hyman would spend their time down in the barn sipping cider, talking in Yiddish and sometimes taking shots of whisky from the stash with which Sam Bronfman clandestinely provided Herschel.

ELEVEN

"May your coming be in peace; . . . Bless me for peace; . . . May your departure be to peace . . ."
"Shalom Aleicheim"--The liturgical poem from the Kabbalists of Safed

Today, Hershel is a worldly man whose years in this country have practically eliminated any trace of an Eastern European accent from his English. He still speaks Yiddish, but it has become Americanized, using w's instead of v's and avoiding guttural ch's and r's. His outlook is also modern. He reads newspapers like the New York Times and periodicals like the New Republic and the National Review. He and his wife travel the world together before she dies. Living on a huge farm in Mentor does not make him provincial.

Though not his chief interest, his farm accustoms him to finance and the commodities market. It has also left him with sophisticated banking connections and a set of influential political friends. He knows how to read the futures market, which requires his attention in planning his annual crops. He's also aware of sophisticated organizational and managerial techniques, because he prefers the role of gentleman farmer to that of a hands-on farmer. This leaves him time to pursue various charitable activities to which he has grown accustomed because of the contacts he has made through the years, contacts with people like the Bronfmans of Canada, Abba Hillel Silver of the United Jewish Appeal in Cleveland, and Eliezer Kaplan of the International Jewish Agency for Palestine. In short, he is a sophisticated individual who is acquainted with many important people. It was not, however, always this way. Certainly not when he and Pa first became friends. Herschel Bloom is also a down to earth man, *haimish*, as he would be called in Yiddish. which is, perhaps, the major reason why it is possible for Hyman Zeltzer and him to be such close friends.

It is a Sunday, and I am driving up from Akron, Ohio to the Bloom farm near Lake Erie. The trip takes about an hour and a half, and it gives me time to think how to handle an interview concerning my father with Mr. Bloom. As perhaps Pa's closest friend, Bloom would not take kindly to indelicacies on my part. But how does one ask a family friend about a two-year gap in the relationship between one's father and mother, actually two and a half years?

How does a child ask an outsider, thirty-seven years his elder, who is a non-family member, about the personal relationship between the child's parents? Of course the explanations for Pa's two-year absence could be many, and not necessarily have anything to do with the personal relationship of a husband and his wife. There could have been an illness, maybe a mental illness. There could have been an emergency. Maybe there was drinking. Maybe there was a misunderstanding. Perhaps Pa had committed a crime.

Why, even now, could my mother not talk about it? Why, back then, while it was happening, did she blithely dodge my questions about what was going on? Of course it could also have been something a child, even as an adult, would prefer not to think about.

I stop for breakfast, a doughnut and some coffee, at a diner. There, gazing out the plate glass window, watching the trucks go by, what I will do and say when I see Herschel Bloom comes to me. I will not simply ask where my father was and what he was doing during the first two years after World War Two. Nor will I reveal that my mother really can't, or doesn't want to, talk to me about it. I will simply ask him to tell me in English "the old stories" --*Da Alt Geshikhtem* he and Pa used to discuss in Yiddish and laugh about down in the barn as they were drinking when my wife and my boys were visiting the farm years ago. Perhaps the answer to my questions lay within them. If the Old Stories don't yield the information I'm looking for, only then will I ask him point blank if he knew where my father was during his absences between June 1946 and April 1948.

There are only three answers he can give. *I don't know. I can't or won't talk about it. Or the true answer.* Of course, then I'll have to ask myself, what if the true answer is something I don't like? How will I relate to that?

I knew I could handle the answer if it related to something negative about my deceased father. My feelings about him were all pretty well set by now. To me he was a distant man, not much of a father, and mostly, an uneducated immigrant from Russia. There might be disappointment, but I could move on from there.

But what if the answer revealed something negative about my mother? Or what if it related to something negative about my brother? I did not consider Ma to be distant, and certainly not uneducated. And despite his mistakes and his illness, I did not harbor the same kind of feelings about Ben as I did about Pa. Ben was, after all, my older brother, and for that reason alone perhaps somebody to be looked up to. Besides, I was still living with these people and I would have to do so for a long time.

Then, of course, there was the real question. Why was I even bothering to care at this point? Maybe I, myself, am sick. Maybe I have OCD and I am obsessing on something not worth the effort.

Arriving at the farm I'm shocked to find how old and frail Bloom now looks. He has a caretaker, Jaida, an older woman from Jamaica who speaks English well. She wheels him out onto the porch as I arrive. He cannot rise to greet me, and the caretaker helps him as I bend down across his wheelchair to hug him. Tears wet a corner of his eye as he hugs back. Jaida dries them away.

"De are tears from rembrance of everyting," she offers, "or maybe he jess miss your Papa."

Bloom and I then go through the initial salutations one would expect between a contemporary of one's parents and the child of the parents following the passage of years without seeing each other. "How is your mother," he asks, "and your children and wife—oh and your brother?" Finishing these amenities, he comes straight to the point.

"So tell me, I received your letter saying that since I couldn't make it to the funeral you wanted to come to see me, but I sense there is also another reason why you have come. Am I correct?"

"Yes, I've come to ask you some questions about my father, to help me fill in some gaps in my knowledge about him."

"Oh, well then this could take some time," he answers tongue in cheek. "If you want to know who someone is, you must ask what he's done. One could ask how your father and I ever became friends. After all, anyone who knows us knows we are very different. But he taught me a lot with his simple straight-forward approach. Things I never would have learned elsewhere, things like money, though important, is just a salve that one can rub into one's wounds to make himself feel better, not a substitute for actually giving of one' s time and body or actually being there to help others. Things like no price can really be put on loyalty. Without loyalty a friend is merely an acquaintance. The number of true friends a person has can usually be counted on one hand, he used to say."

Herschel then attests to his love for my father and apologizes for not being able to attend his funeral. He glances down at the wheelchair where he sits. "Diabetes can really be cruel when it plagues you with its neuropathies," he says. "The pain becomes excruciating, constantly requiring one to change his position. It's not good for long rides in cars." Then he shifts in the wheelchair uncomfortably.

"Easy to think that your father was a simple man," he continues. "Right? But he wasn't. I knew him well. In fact, he was very complex, and he lived by a code from which he never strayed. It was the result of growing up in a large Russian family of girls with only one brother, who though a virtuoso, was a very weak person. It was also the result of his education at the Synagogue in Kherson, where he had to struggle with his lessons and never excelled. Excuse me while I become a psychiatrist for a little while. Just remember I'm no Sigmund Freud." He smiles. "First let me give you a little background on Hymie. Without his backstory it's difficult to understand who a man really was."

"His brother seemed to everyone like a *mensch,*" Bloom goes on. "I never met his brother, but Hymie convinced me everyone back in Kherson thought the brother was a wonderful guy, whereas their impression of Hymie was that he was little more than a strong ox—a *bulvan.* if you will. Neither of these impressions were true. The brother was weak and self-centered. Hymie, was big and strong like an ox, but an ox who always tried to do the right thing. He was not crude. He wasn't loud and he wasn't classless 'You do the right thing because it's the right thing to do and for no other reason,' he would say. 'Help comes only to those who try to help themselves.' That was one of his favorite bromides. And he was also religious. 'If you don't forget God, He won't forget you. So read Torah and go to *Schul.*' That was the basic thing he got out of his education. Study Torah."

"But at Pa's funeral, the Rabbi said he was no great scholar in school."

"I didn't say he was a scholar. I said he was religious. I'm sure he choked on things like the *Mishnah* during his Jewish education. To him nothing was more esoteric than

93

the Talmud. He could never get through it during his classes. But the man was spiritual. Once, he and I discussed how the Holocaust could have ever happened, and he says to me, 'I don't know. It's like once God's light filled the whole universe, and he put some of it into separate vessels to make mankind, but the vessels shattered into thousands of pieces, and now it's our job to collect them and fix them.'

"Years later, I realized he was expressing the *Kabbalistic* idea of a man's responsibility to repair the world. We Jews call it *Tikkun Olam,*--the idea that the world is made up of good and evil, and in order for the balance between the two intended by God to be kept up, humans must be involved in the world's restoration and repair. He didn't bother himself about the "why" of the Holocaust, only about what he was supposed to do about it in order to do the right thing, in order to perfect the world under God's reign." It's mystical. Where he got this idea from, I don't know. All I know is that I read it once in the writings of Maimonides, one of our greatest Torah scholars.

"Hmph, that's very strange, but it does sound like Pa. Often he'd say, 'do it because it's the right thing to do.' I always thought he said this because he was so stubborn. Tell me, did you find him to be as stubborn a man, as I did?

"Oh yes, that was very much a part of the *bulvan,* in him, if you will. He was stubborn as an ox, as the saying goes. But mostly, stubborn when he was right and others were wrong."

"Drifting from thought to thought, as Bloom was, I can see that we'll not get to what I really want to know unless I channel his thinking. So decide I need to point him in the right direction. I hope I can do it delicately.

"Mr. Bloom. Tell me the Old Stories in English, will you? *Da Alt Geshikhtem.*"

Bloom shifts again in his wheelchair. He clears his throat, giving me a quizzical look. "All of them," he asks?

Hoping he doesn't ask me why I want to know, I reply,

"As many of them as you can."

"Well I hope you brought your pajamas with you," he jokes, "because it's going to take a few days. *Da Alt Geshikhtem,* as your mother used to refer to them, are really old remembrances."

"Remembrances of what?" I ask. It sounds like this is a mistake and that we're about to embark on a tangent that's not going to reveal where my father was between 1946 and 1948.

"Remembrances of things that very few people know anything about," Bloom says. "Things that very little has been written about. But things that are very important in history, although not talked about by many people very specifically.

"They're not going to mean anything to you unless I start from the very beginning. I can't just jump into the middle of the stories with a story here and a story there, because you won't understand. They have been kept secret for a long time, secret in some parts even from your mother and from my former wife—blessed memory."

"Ok, then let's start from the beginning," I say. "If I have to, I'll go out and buy some pajamas in Mentor. Do *Da Alt Geshikhtem* involve World War Two?"

"Yes and no."

TWELVE

"And if those ships are illegal, so was the Boston Tea Party."

"Underground to Palestine" I. F. Stone

Jaida brings tea and cake to us on the porch. Herschel thanks her and settles back to light his pipe. A look of disapproval crosses her face as he strikes his match.

Herschel looks up at her. "Oh, now Jaida, smoking this pipe will only take milliseconds off my life," he assures her. Then, he looks at me with a question in his eye. I can see he doesn't know where to begin.

"The old stories?" He says. "To understand them, first you'll need a short history lesson, but we need not go back very far. Think Hitler. Think Holocaust. Think of the end of World War Two. Then think of your father."

"But my father wasn't in World War Two," I tell him. "He was right here in America during the war."

"Yes, but only until after the fighting in Europe ended. Then, one day after the war in Europe ends, he comes to me and he says he wants to help the Jewish refugees in the displaced person camps, because maybe there are members of his own family in those camps. I tell him that its very commendable . . ." Bloom pauses. He interrupts himself . . . "Oh what the heck," he splutters. "That's not the way to start. Maybe the best way to begin is actually to jump right into the middle."

He's confusing me a lot, but I'm encouraged by his statement about the end of the fighting in Europe. Not until after VE day, I presume he means, but the war continued

96

after that with Japan into August 1945, which is about when Pa began to disappear. Maybe we're actually getting on the track of where he was between 1946 and 1948.

"Ever hear of the Jew's Secret Fleet," Bloom asks, expecting me to draw a blank on the question? "Well, your father and I knew all about it."

He observes my puzzlement with a gleam, as if he thinks I think he's crazy. "It had ten boats in it, well ships, or whatever you want to call them, all from North America: The Wedgewood, The Arlosoroff, The Ben Hecht, The Hatikva, The Pan York, The Pan Crescent, The Haganah, The Geula, The Jewish State, and The Exodus. There was an eleventh called the Calanit, but it was not considered part of the fleet because it delivered refugees to Israel only after Israel became an independent state."

I continue drawing the blank he expected.

"Ever hear of the Exodus," He asks.

"Of course I have! You mean the refugee boat Leon Uris wrote about, or are you talking about some other ship that's been in the Israeli Navy?"

The former, although some of the boats in the Jew's Secret Fleet, not the Exodus, ultimately wound up in Israel's navy too. Let me think. Uh, I believe The Wedgewood, The Haganah, The Ben Hecht, and The Jewish State all later turned up in Israel's Navy."

"Mr. Bloom, what are we talking about here? I'll admit it. I don't understand. I mean I learned on the day of his funeral that my father had been in the Russian Navy, but a Jewish Secret Fleet? I've never heard anything about that."

Now Bloom is laughing. "Well that's what *Da Alt Geshikhtem* are about, the Jew's Secret Fleet. You see. Your father and I were once on the Hatikva, which was in the Jewish Secret Fleet."

"What?"

"You heard me. Chaim and I were on the Hatikvah, one of the ships in the Jewish Secret Fleet."

"So where did these boats you speak of come from? I've never heard of the Secret Jewish Fleet.""

"They were all bought either at scrap or for war surplus prices and refitted. Let me see." He pauses to think and begins counting down on his fingers. "Two were Canadian war boats, one was a Coast Guard revenue cutter during prohibition, another was just a Coast Guard boat, another was a Coast Guard training boat, another was a . . . oh yes, a Coast Guard icebreaker, two were Banana carriers, one was a private yacht used for smuggling purposes, and one was a presidential yacht, originally called the Mayflower, used by Presidents Theodore Roosevelt through Herbert Hoover."

I reach for a piece of cake and settle back into my chair wondering if we should even continue this conversation. Either Bloom has a little dementia, or this is going to be a long day—maybe both. "OK, tell me about the Jew's Secret Fleet." I've decided to humor him.

"I will, but first you need to know about *Ha'pala* and the *Aliyah Bet*. Ha'pala means "ascension," or literally "to go up." It's the term used by Zionists and Israelis for the immigration of Jews to Israel. Today, in America when we say 'to make Aliyah' it also means to immigrate to Israel. *Aliyah Bet* was a code word used between 1939 and 1948 to signify the illegal immigration by Jews to Palestine when it was still a territory carved out of the former Ottoman Empire after World War One and administered by a mandate to the British to govern the area."

"But why was it illegal for Jews to immigrate to Palestine? I thought Britain's Balfour Declaration called for a Jewish National Home in the territory of Palestine.

"It did, but the Arabs didn't like that idea, so in 1936 they threw a few riots and a general strike, which the British saw as an Arab revolt. The Brits then came up with the idea of partitioning Palestine into a Jewish state and an Arab state in order to end conflict between the Arabs and the Zionists. The Arabs absolutely hated that idea and the Zionists were ambivalent about it, especially after a deep split in their ranks between those who just wanted all of Palestine to be a separate Jewish country and those who only wanted a Jewish enclave in part of Palestine for a Jewish national home.

"Then World War II broke out and the Brits decided their interests were best served by pleasing the Arabs, so they issued the "White Paper" which limited Jewish immigration to Palestine to 75,000 over 5 years, and ruled that the amount of further immigration thereafter was to be determined by the Arab majority. It also put restrictions on the rights of Jews to buy land from Arabs. All this while still paying lip service to the idea of a Jewish National Home in an independent Palestinian state within 10 years. The White Paper was issued by the government of Neville Chamberlain and approved by the House of Commons. As you know, the government of Neville Chamberlain was full of chicken-shits. Remember the Munich accord with Hitler? Peace in our time? Humph! That's when the *Aliyah Bet* got started."

Despite Herschel's colorful speech, I feared this was a history lesson that was about to get as boring as Sunday School. I had half observed all this by reading the newspapers as it was happening, but since I wasn't a Zionist I didn't care a hoot about it at the time. And I never read anything about any Secret Fleet of the Jews.

"Well what did the so-called 'Secret Fleet of the Jews' have to do with any of this." I asked? "I repeat. I've never heard of it. I've read things about this period at the time it was occurring, but frankly I wasn't that interested."

"Well your father was. When the allies found the Nazi concentration camps in 1945 at the end of the war and threw open their gates, thousands of refugees staggered out, many of them Jews who were not welcomed back to their former homes in Europe, especially Eastern Europe. At the time, immigration to the Americas had become greatly restricted because we were just getting over the Great Depression. So about 150,000 Jewish survivors of the horrors of the

99

Holocaust remained bottled up in displaced person camps with nowhere to go but to Palestine. Because of continued Arab pressure, the new British Labor Government dragged its feet on the issue, refusing to open the Palestinian territories to higher immigration quotas than permitted by the White Paper of Chamberlain's government.

"So suddenly, your father, who never before evidenced any feeling toward the Palestine situation, and who was always negative about Zionism, becomes an ardent Zionist. That was my opinion, not his. He always claimed not to be a Zionist. Having left almost his entire family back in Europe, and having a wife in the same shoes, does not seem to me like it's enough to account for his change of heart because so many years have passed since he's seen his siblings. Nonetheless, he comes to me and says he's very concerned about these refugees and he wants to do something to help get them to Palestine.

"It's a Zionist cause," I caution him. "Remember? Many times before you have said you don't understand Zionism and you don't see why anyone would want to immigrate to a desert."

"Then you can call me a Zionist now, if that's what you must call me," he announces. "You can say to yourself, now he understands, if that's what you must say to yourself. Hitler has made me understand. There is no chance for a good life for Jews anywhere in Europe."

"This turn-around is startling," Bloom says, "practically unexplainable if you've heard him discuss the subject before, as I had. Whereas before he was loathed to part with even a dollar of his money for the Jewish causes, now he's champing at the bit to do something. I tell myself I must remember, he can only read in Yiddish, and the Yiddish newspaper in Cleveland is filled with horror stories about the Jewish DPs in Europe. But that also doesn't seem like enough to explain the sudden reversal in his thinking. He tells me that over the years he's saved up $3000 dollars, and he wants to contribute that now. I tell him that it's very commendable that he wants to do something to help, but $3000 is not going to go very far.

"Perhaps you should just keep saving and give it all to your grandchildren if you want to do something for somebody. Give it to them for their college educations."

"What you're really saying is that having $3000 is like having no money at all, that it's not good enough," Hymie protests.

"No, no," I answer fearing I've insulted him. "What I'm saying is that you can do more by helping in other ways, giving of your time to the cause, going around and speaking about it to others, maybe working in the Jewish Appeal office for free, or even helping to pack and mail items needed right now by the refugees to the DP camps in Europe."

"No," he replies stubbornly. "Once you told me that if I have no money to contribute to these organizations, then I can contribute my time, but that's not good enough I think. Now you're telling me my money's not good enough, and I'm telling you that the way you say I should contribute my time is not good enough either."

"Hymie, if that's how you feel, I don't know what to say," I tell him.

"Once you told me that arrangements are being made by these Jewish organizations to buy ships to carry Jewish refugees to Palestine. People are needed to help with these plans. I want to go on one of those ships and help bring the refugees to Palestine."

"Hymie" I say. "That's ridiculous. It's illegal and it would be dangerous. I don't think that's something you should do, or that you even can do."

"Why not," he challenges? "I'm a machinist, I even once worked in shipyards, doing this work on ships. I know the work. I'm also a sailor. I once sailed in battles fought by the Russian Navy."

David Selcer

"Hymie, how old were you when you did that? Sixteen, seventeen?"

"So what? Why shouldn't I be able to contribute the best things I know how to do? I can still do this."

"But look at you today. You're in your fifties now. This is ridiculous."

"Suddenly there's silence," Bloom says. "I watch the huge bear of a man in front of me cast his eyes toward the floor, and after a long moment of contemplation look up. The eyes are now like a child's eyes, pleading, almost tearing, resolute, ashamed. *Have I insulted him again?*

"Then I realize what he's thinking. These are the eyes of a once strapping young man with a trade, who has fended for himself, alone, through all sorts of adversity for his first twenty-five years of life, crossing Russia, crossing the Pacific Ocean, crossing Canada and reaching the United States, only to play second fiddle for the next twenty-five years of his life to his wife."

I begin to understand what Bloom is saying, or at least I think I do. Though a wonderful person, Ma has enabled Pa to lead a comfortable middle class life, with little responsibility, in a grocery business she has been able to make a "go" of because of her education, her intellect, her charm, and her ability to read and write in five languages, all things Pa does not have and cannot do by himself. It wasn't his doing. It was hers. I begin to think, maybe he's just gotten tired of playing second fiddle and he wanted to come into his own; to assert himself, so to speak, to do something on his own.

Or, maybe he just wanted out. Maybe he wanted to feel he was accomplishing something on his own by making a difference, changing the world a little, doing something different. Maybe he just wanted something a little more exciting than selling fruit from a truck, stocking a grocery store and playing cards with friends. Maybe he was tired of keeping the store clean and stacking canned goods for

102

display. I know the feeling because when I worked there, I felt the same. I wanted to deal with more worldly concerns, with far more exciting things. But Bloom steers my focus in another direction when he says:

"Hymie," I ask him. "What's the real reason you want to do this?"

"Because it's the right thing to do," he answers. "Because it's the right thing to do. And you should do it too. You should do it with me. We are both too fat and happy sitting here on our asses." He lets out one of his uncontrollable bursts of laughter. He covers his mouth with his hand trying to suppress the laughter without much success, and says, "Please excuse my English but I think it's time to do something about the situation. People are going to die in those DP camps if something isn't done, just like they did in the concentration camps, but without any bullets or gas. That will be the only difference."

"So tell me Hymie. When did you become such a Zionist?" I tease.

Hymie sighs and says, "I don't know what a Zionist is, but if it's something political, which I think it could be, I don't believe in it. What I do believe in is that I must somehow help to change the future of the Jewish people, or someday, there will be no Jews left except us here in this country. I should help repair the problem, and you should do it too. So alright, it's not enough to give the little money I have. Who knows what that will accomplish, but if I can actually know that I am saving just one life, that will satisfy me."

I couldn't imagine Pa being a Zionist. I couldn't imagine him being a philosopher. I couldn't imagine him having any interests other than in the basest needs for survival, enough food to eat, a good bed to sleep in, and a good wife, like my mother, to take care of him. Mostly, I couldn't imagine him as being any sort of idealist or scholar. Yet his pronouncement to Bloom, that if he could know that he was actually saving one life it would satisfy him, reminded me of something I'd read recently about a tractate in the *Mishnah* that said, "whoever destroys a single life in Israel is considered by Scripture to have destroyed the whole world and whoever saves a single life in Israel is considered by Scripture to have saved the whole world." Had Pa actually learned this precept in school as a boy I wondered?

"So that's the introduction," Mr. Bloom says. "Now here is the first *alt geshikta.* Just settle back and I'll try to make it as interesting as possible for you. It's the story your father and I used to laugh about more than any of the others."

THIRTEEN

"If it stays afloat, I can get it over there."
**--Captain Vigo Thompson, assigned
to ferry _Exodus_ to Europe**

The first story, according to Bloom, begins in March 1946. It starts with the description of a former ship's captain. Captain William C. Ash is a professional mariner, a sea captain and a wartime officer in the U.S. Maritime Service, who served after World War II as port captain for the American Foreign Steamship Corporation until he set up his own business as a marine surveyor with an office in the Wall Street District. A Jew born in Poland, he is also an officer of the Masters, Mates and Pilots Union.

He now sits in an office at 24 Stone Street in Manhattan, the door of which bears the name Weston Trading Company. Weston Trading has been organized to control ships registered in Panama to a Panamanian company called Arias and Arias, so they can sail under the Panamanian flag. Arias and Arias is little more than a mailing address allowing ships of the Secret Fleet of the Jews to sail under a 'flag of convenience' unassociated with the United States. This surreptitious, but completely legal maneuver, is necessary to prevent awkwardness in the United States' relations with Great Britain, which is currently blockading Jews from immigrating to Palestine.

Bloom, who was present at an interview between Captain Ash and my father, begins the first ault Geshikta. He makes it as colorful as he can.

"Recruited by Morris Ginsburg, a member of the family

owning his former employer, the American Foreign Steamship Corporation, Captain Ash," says Bloom, "has become a key figure in the American operations of Aliyah Bet. He is instrumental in buying and equipping vessels that will carry refugees to Palestine. He does so with the contacts, prestige and advice of Ginsburg, an American Zionist who also acts as a financial guarantor and disburses payments for the ships. Additionally, Captain Ash also manages the recruitment and training of volunteers for the crews of the Aliyah Bet ships.

"Behind him stands Aliyah Bet's Palestinian Director of activities in the United States, Ze'ev (Danny) Schind. Shind is a congenial redhead from Kibbutz Ayelet Hashahar who has come to the United States to oversee Aliyah Bet's operations here. Right now, he has a very skeptical look on his face. He can't believe what he is seeing and hearing from the two men in front of him who are applying as crew members for Aliyah Bet's ships. They've travelled to New York from Ohio for this meeting at their own expense.

"I know how to run an engine room," Pa is telling Captain Ash in broken but understandable English. "In fact I could take the whole thing apart and put it back together again for you. I know how to repair any ship's part if it's made from metal, including propellers and rudders. I went to sea with the Russian navy."

"When were you in Russia's navy, "Captain Ash asks, with a tell-tale twinkle of disbelief in his eye?"

"In 1905. But I'm still plenty strong. Oh, and I can speak Yiddish to your passengers when that's needed. That's not something you'll find with many of the people you're interviewing. *Du farshtayn da yiddish shprach?"*

"Ash throws his thumbs back over his shoulders when he hears the year 1905, and he shrugs when asked if he understands Yiddish. 'Now those are points nobody else has made to us,' he says. Nobody's come in here from the 1905 Russian Navy speaking Yiddish and asking to be a part of

Aliyah Bet. But look, Mr. Zeltzer, these boats we're
acquiring are very old and they will be in constant need of
maintenance, although I doubt we'll be picking anything up
going back as far as the 1905 Russian Navy.'
"He smiles and rolls his eyes at Schind. 'Not only will
the trips across the Atlantic be arduous, but when you enter
the Mediterranean basin you will be in constant danger from
the British who will block and harass you with their patrol
boats and destroyers, and try to board you. What makes you
think you can handle all that? What would you do sir?'

"Whatever I am told to do," your Pa says. "Listen, I
have crossed an ocean living in the hold of a freighter once,
and I know about rough seas. I have escaped from a sinking
battleship during wartime. What makes you think I can't do
it?"

"Hymie, *vayzn respekt!*," I tell your father, grabbing his
shoulder.

"I have respect, but I must convince him I can do this."

"But you are too old," Schind finally jumps in. "I'm
sorry to be so blunt, but we will be turning away many more
volunteers than we are accepting, many who are much
younger than you."

"I am too old," Hymie says? "So tell me Mr. Schind,
since you are so young. What do you know about sailing on
a boat? What do you know about how to run an engine
room? What do you know about Yiddish? Not Hebrew but
Yiddish! Do you speak it? All your passengers will. Have
you ever been to sea?"

"Captain Ash looks down at his hands on the desk in
front of him, carefully folding them with his fingers
interlaced. Then he smiles, looking up at Schind. 'One
thing's for sure, Schind. This man's got the moxie for it.'

'He's also got a wife,' Schind protests. 'What about her?
Who will take care of her if he doesn't come back?'

'A wife and two *grown up* children,' Hymie sasses back.
'They're all completely capable of taking care of themselves.'

Bloom then comments, "I hear Hymie saying this, but I know his heart is twinging a little as he says it. I know he's thinking: *What if Ben gets sick again? Can he really take care of himself then?*

"And you, Mr. Schind?" Hymie stubbornly argues back at the twenty-eight-year-old Jew from Palestine. "I suppose you're not married?"

"Actually, I just married. She's an American I met in Palestine."

"*Mazel tov*, We both say together."

"And you, Mr. Bloom, what have you got to say for yourself," Schind asks? It seems he's trying to change the subject. "Why do you want to do this?"

"I want to do it because I am a Zionist who has given a lot of money to Ha'pala and Aliyah Bet, and now I want to see my money in action."

Bloom also says, "I want to go because Hymie here has convinced me of what I'm sure you already know, that just giving money is not good enough. One must give of oneself."

"And you think that's a good enough reason to sail on an Aliyah Bet ship," the Palestinian scoffs. "Well I'm not sure it is. This is going to be very dangerous work."

Bloom says he scoffed back, saying, "Tell me Mr. Schind. You Palestinians, you all come over here to the U.S: Reuven Zalansky, with his talk of organizing a Haganah military force, Jacob Dostovsky who comes to mobilize American Jewish support, Eliezer Kaplan of the Jewish Agency for Palestine, David Ben-Gurion, Chaim Weizmann, and you, yourself. And you all tell us we should make Aliyah to Palestine. Hmm!

"Dangerous you say. Well if I'm good enough to make Aliyah to Palestine, where there's probably going to be a fight for survival with the Arabs, according to Mr. Ben-Gurion, then why am I not also good enough for Aliyah Bet? It's just as dangerous living in Palestine. And besides that,

I'm sure not everyone you're going to choose to crew ships for Aliyah Bet has had experience at sea. Am I right? So why am I not just like those you will choose who have no such experience?"

"All that is true Mr. Bloom. But you could wind up in a foreign jail if you work for Aliyah Bet. You might also lose your life."

"Well I could also lose my life just living in Palestine! Is that not true?"

"Alright," Ash says, standing up from his desk to terminate the conversation. That's enough for now. We will take both your applications under advisement, and we will let you know."

"When?" Hymie asks?

"Within two months. But there is much to do before then. Much more than just recruiting crew members. I must find ships capable of carrying large numbers of refugees. This I can do on the "hush-hush" with the handful of high level business contacts Mr. Schind here has acquired in this country, all of whom are discreet, and all of whom know how to find used vessels for sale at prices we can afford.

"We need not tell the sellers of these vessels why we're buying them, you see. We need not mention Aliyah Bet or our intention to run the British blockade of Palestine with the boats we're purchasing. All we have to do is find the boats and negotiate the price. It can all be done quietly and discreetly.

"But recruiting crews is a whole different story. I must find sea captains and men capable of navigating, handling a sextant and steering a ship, not just men capable of running an engine room. Hopefully, I have the contacts needed for this, although I am sure not all the people I find will be Jewish. I plan to engage non-Jewish captains, if necessary, to take the boats across the Atlantic and then replace them with volunteer Jewish Palestinian commanders for the rest of the trip across the Mediterranean to Europe and then to

Palestine.

"At the very least, all the captains and first mates I find must fit two requirements: 1) dependability to do their shipboard jobs under difficult conditions; and 2) dependability to keep what we are doing secret. And there will be little or no pay for them. Hopefully, I can find able professional Jewish seamen like this among the Merchant Marine, who will work for a good cause for next to nothing. You know 10 % of America's merchant fleet is currently made up of Jews. I don't think anybody knows that. They may be Jews in name only who have never stepped inside a synagogue. But they're Jews.

"As for the rest of the sailors we need, the deck hands, Mr. Bloom, you should know that the men we choose who are not accomplished at piloting, navigating or the other seaman's trades, will be swabbing decks, chipping paint and, cleaning, cooking and carrying out a myriad of other functions that common sailors do. It's often dirty backbreaking work.

"Furthermore, I can't just go to the seamen's hiring halls like a commercial vessel's captain would, and publicize the need for Aliyah Bet crews without telling applicants what Aliyah Bet crews will be doing. I can't tell common sailors applying from the seaman's hiring halls what they will really be doing because we're an underground organization in no position to publicize our purpose. I cannot tell them they'll be picking up refugees from Europe and smuggling them to Palestine.

"What if there are informants in the hiring halls who tell the British of our plans? That will end our mission before it even begins because the British will protest our intentions to the State Department. You've heard the phrase 'loose lips sink ships,' I'm sure. Well, the loosest lips you'll find are in the seaman's hiring halls. Our operations must be kept clandestine. So where do I go to get common sailors?

"And by the way, Mr. Bloom, you should understand

that the only reason I agreed to let you and Mr. Zeltzer come here to see me is because the Canadian, Samuel Bronfman, insisted that I give you an audience and that you could be trusted. You and Mr. Zeltzer cannot go out and talk about what has been said in this office today. We are a secret organization that's mission must be kept quiet at all costs."

Schind raises his fore finger to his lips and says "sh, shhhh" to underscore what Ash is saying.

"Try the Zionist Youth Organizations," I tell him.

"The what," asks Captain Ash?

"The Zionist Youth groups that are a part of the American Zionist organizations. They're all highly motivated; they're, discreet, and they have their own channels of communication. Many of their members have gone on to serve in the armed services and are now freshly back from World War II. They know of young Jewish war veterans who might be interested in your mission even though they know nothing about sailing on ships. They will also be interested in volunteering to go themselves for no pay, except maybe pocket money for cigarettes, because they want to make Aliyah to Palestine and to be of service along the way. Much of the program of the Zionist Youth Groups involves preparing to make Aliyah to Palestine."

"Thank you for your suggestions Mr. Bloom. We will also take them under advisement."

"Yes, thank you," Danny Schind chimes in. "There is an organization called Palestine Vocational Services. I think they've been in contact the Zionist youth groups. If not, I can make sure that happens."

Bloom goes on to explain how, after thanking Captain Ash for seeing them and leaving the interview, they assume that after the door closes behind them, Schind will turn to Ash and say, "So in six weeks or so, you'll write them both a letter telling them no. Right?"

Bloom says, "Outside the door, I turn to Hymie and say, "I don't know how well that went in there. They just think we're too old."

Hymie replies, "I'm sure that Palestinian 'shoosh-shah boy' is in there right now telling him 'no.'"

"I told you Hymie. We're too old."

But Hymie replies, "We'll see."

FOURTEEN

"Boys, don't go getting involved in any of them foreign wars in the Middle East."
--Chesapeake Bay harbor pilot to departing Aliyah Bet sailors

"So tell me what happened," I say. "I really can't believe they took you into Aliyah Bet? Don't tell me *da alt geshickhtem* are truly all about the days the two of you spent in an Aliyah Bet boat together! I know you said before that you were on one of their boats, but I really can't believe it was on an actual Aliyah Bet mission."

Bloom lights another pipe and smiles. "What happened," he says? "Nothing happened, at least nothing predictable. When we met with Ash and Schind, something called the Anglo-American Committee of Inquiry, composed of diplomats, politicians and professors, was simultaneously discussing the problem of Jewish immigration to the former Ottoman territory then known as British Mandatory Palestine. The Committee met in Washington and in London, travelled to the DP camps in Europe to get the Holocaust survivor's views on where they wanted to live, and then to Cairo to get the Arab viewpoint. The problem was, you see, that both the Jews and the Arabs wanted Palestine for their own country.

"Among other things, the Committee wound up recommending in April 1946 that 100,000 Jews be allowed to leave the European DP camps and immigrate to Mandatory Palestine immediately; and that the former British 'White Paper' rules preventing Jews from buying

113

land there be rescinded. The war now being over, Great
Britain said it would accept these recommendations if the
United States would provide financial aid and commit troops
to help Britain provide security assistance in case there was
another Arab revolt over the matter."

He interrupts himself, calling to his care-taker. "Jaida,
would you please bring me that scrap book from the shelf
with the glass cover doors in the office?" Jaida delivers a
tattered green book to us that is so old its spine is broken and
there is string tied around it to keep its front and back covers
together. Then he goes back to the story.

"President Truman endorses everything in the Report of
the Anglo-American Committee of Inquiry, but he refuses to
help the British provide security with American troops. That
never gets approved. So Britain rejects the report and goes
back to its White Paper policy restricting Jewish emigration
and land purchases. In the meantime, your father and I travel
around the Mid-west from Kansas City to Chicago to
Toronto, Canada and Buffalo, New York attending Zionist
functions and speaking about what happened at the Twenty-
Second Zionist Congress in Basil, Switzerland in July 1946.
At that Congress, for the first time, the Zionists formally call
for the establishment of a separate independent Jewish State
in the Mandatory Palestinian territories, and they refuse to
attend a Palestine Conference called by the British for
October 1, 1946, instead deciding to try to put pressure on
the UN to do something.

"Up until then, everything but a separate country has
been proposed for the Jews in Mandatory Palestine. The
proposals include, during World War One, an amorphous
'national Jewish home' in territory lost by the old Ottoman
Empire, and after World War II, a country that is neither a
Jewish nor an Arab state, moving under British governance
toward self-government with equal rights for everyone and
international guarantees to protect the rights of the three
Abrahamic faiths in the area. A third proposal is later made

for a federation of self-ruled Jewish and Arab provinces overseen by the British with Britain in direct control of Jerusalem and the Negev. But the Arabs fear this would lead to the partition of Palestine. So they reject it. In fact, all of these proposals are rejected by either the Arabs, the Jews or both.

"So later, in October 1946, the Brits decide on their own to gradually allow 96,000 Jews to emigrate to Palestine at the rate of 1,500 a month over slightly more than 5 years. Half these Jews are refugees who have already attempted to enter Palestine illegally and are being held on the island of Cyprus as illegal immigrants after they were stopped. You see, the British feared an uprising by the Jewish refugees on Cyprus, just as much as they feared another Arab uprising in Palestine.

"At about that time your father and I both receive letters saying the same thing." Bloom then unties the string carefully and opens the tattered scrap book Jaida has delivered, slowly turning over its pages. "Ah, here it is," he says, "my copy of the letter." He takes out a letter written on the stationery of the Weston Trading Company in New York and reads:

'Dear Mr. Bloom:

A vessel purchased in Canada has been refitted and is scheduled to sail from Miami in February, 1947 to Baltimore, where it will take on crew members. From Baltimore it will depart for Europe. The name of the ship is Tradewinds. It is registered in Panama. If you are still interested in serving as a crew member, please sign the agreement you will receive under separate cover in a few days and return it to the Post Office Box number and address thereon by November 10, 1946.

Please also be at the Baltimore, Maryland Sailors' Hall

by no later than 3:00 p.m. on February 10, 1947, at which time you will be apprised of the billet arrangements that have been made for you until the ship sales.

Very truly yours,

Dewey Stone'

Bloom carefully turns a few more pages in the scrap book; pulls out a half-sheet with a Washington D.C post office address on it; and says, "Here's my copy of the agreement we signed."

'I hereby agree to serve on the ship known as Tradewinds, sailing under the flag of Panama from Baltimore, MD, without pay, other than pocket money. I understand that there is no time limit as to the duration of the voyage, and that I may not discuss its destination with anyone, including my family. I further agree before sailing to be sworn into the Haganah and to subject myself to Haganah discipline thereafter.'

"Your father and I both signed this agreement and we travelled to Baltimore together on the Baltimore & Ohio Railroad in February 1947. As you know, the Haganah later became the army of Israel."

"Oh my God," I say! "You both joined Aliyah Bet! How old were the both of you then?"

Bloom starts laughing. "Oh my God is right. Never mind how old we were. The <u>Tradewinds</u> was really old. She almost didn't make it from Miami to Baltimore. She hit bad weather and mechanical trouble when her evaporators failed, and she had to put into Charleston for repairs. When we first laid eyes on her at the Baltimore docks, we were aghast.

"Formerly used as an ice breaker in the St. Lawrence River, the warn out ship looked like she couldn't make it across the Atlantic. We were told that before her service on

116

the St. Lawrence, she'd been a Coast Guard cutter during World War II named the Gresham, patrolling off the coast of Nova Scotia, but we found that difficult to believe. She was practically a scow."

"Wait a minute," I say. "I thought you said you and Pa were on the <u>Hatikva</u>."

"The <u>Tradewinds</u> was later renamed <u>Hatikva</u> while she was at sea. But I'll get to that in another story. Suffice it to say, when we first saw her, her name was <u>Tradewinds</u>.

"Our disbelief when we first saw her, however, was no match for the disbelief we saw in the eyes of her captain, Frank Stanton, when he first looked at us. Stanton is a non-Jew hired to take the <u>Tradewinds</u> to Europe, and there turn it over to a commander from the Palestinian Haganah. He had expected a professional group of sailors to meet him in Baltimore, not our motley crew. When he asks how many of us are qualified as professional mariners, only four hands go up. We later learn from these guys, who'd brought the boat up from Miami, that they are very dubious about her condition.

"'How many of you are navy veterans who've at least been to sea?' Nine more hands go up, including, I might add, your father's hand. 'Well, that's fourteen. I'm not going to even ask about the other seven of you.' he says."

Bloom went on to describe how the crew learned what to do and what not to do. He talks about a former navy officer assigned to load the hold, a job he'd never done, who doesn't know how to set it up so the boxes will not shift at sea. He also describes a fight that starts in a waterfront bar over an anti-Semitic insult, despite warnings not to do anything that might call attention to the crew or its upcoming secret voyage.

"How many of you New York Hymies are in here," the insulter, a local from Baltimore, asks a young volunteer Zionist Youth Groups member? The Zionist invites the insulter to step outside as fierce-looking supporters of each begin moving toward the door, but the confrontation never comes off. Instead, one of the drunken locals slips and falls, knocking himself out. All of the volunteers depart before the police arrive, but not before a Jewish Palestinian "shush-shah" boy, who's a crew member, berates us for drawing attention to themselves.

"And your father," Bloom continues, "he doesn't even know what's going on, or that calling a person a Hymie is an anti-Semitic slur. He just wants to get back to the ship so he can sleep, because the next day he plans to run tests in the engine room."

Bloom also tells a story about how the Tradewinds begins sinking at her moorings in the Baltimore Harbor one day when one of the volunteers connects a water hose to the ship's tanks from a street hydrant. Two good looking female passersby suddenly distract him long enough to draw him into a conversation about them with another crew member. The ogling volunteer is so enthused by the sight of these women that he forgets to turn off the water, which overflows the tanks and floods the ship, soaking blankets, bathrooms and the dining mess room. We had just cleaned it, but our captain makes us do it all again.

His final story is about a Chesapeake Bay pilot who comes aboard to guide the Tradewinds through the harbor and out into the bay beyond. Surmising that the crew is overwhelmingly Jewish, the pilot tells a ship's officer, named Carruthers, "You know Mr. Carruthers, I've been noticing things, and I think this must be one of them Jew ships. You can make yourself a bundle of money on this one."

Actually, Carruthers, the son of a rabbi, who is using the name as a pseudonym, tells the pilot he's mistaken, without telling him mistaken about what. "Was he mistaken about the entire crew being Jewish, or was he mistaken that Carruthers was a Jew, not a gentile like the pilot," Bloom asks? In any event, it becomes clear that the pilot means no harm. As he departs the ship at the mouth of the Harbor and the Chesapeake Bay, he shows his true concern for the sailors on the Tradewinds to a handful of them, including your father by saying, 'Boys don't go getting into any of them foreign wars in the Middle East.'"

"That was good advice," your father tells me years later. "And we should have taken it."

"Why did he feel that way," I ask?

"Because Hymie, if he ever truly was a Zionist at all, was not what we call a Revisionist Zionist or a Revolutionary Zionist. He was closer to being what's called a practical Zionist.

"The revisionists, led by Ze'ev Jabotinsky believed that the historical heritage of the Jewish people in the area of Palestine was the basis for the Zionist national idea; that the establishment of a Jewish State was necessary; and, that firm military action must be taken against the Arab gangs attacking the Jewish Community in Palestine. The Revolutionary Zionists see Zionism as a struggle to ingather Jews from the Diaspora; revive the Hebrew language as a spoken vernacular; and reestablish a Jewish kingdom. To do this, they feel guerilla warfare against the British administration of Palestine is necessary, to end Britain's Mandate and pave the way for Jewish political independence. All of this was too ephemeral and academic—way above your father's ability to conceive or understand, and maybe he was correct to reject these concepts.

"Practical Zionists like your father were molded by the Russian and Polish Hovevei Zion movement which, because of the pogroms, aimed to promote Jewish immigration to Palestine and advance Jewish settlement there, particularly agricultural settlements. Most of them stayed away from politics. Never mind lofty ideals. They believe the Jews just need a new place to go where they can be left alone to live their lives. Their opinion was that the principal thing to do

was to promote the settlement of Palestinian land with
Jewish emigrants as soon as possible, even if a charter over
the Land was not obtained. Your father fit this group
because he wanted to save Jewish refugees in Europe by
getting them to Palestine, which he thought was the only
place left for them to go. I believe he once told me he had an
uncle who felt the same way. Your father had no grandiose
ideas about re-establishing a Jewish Kingdom over
ingathered exiles from the diaspora, and no real appreciation
of any Jewish heritage outside the Pale of Settlement in
Russia where he grew up. Most of all, he did not believe that
violence or terrorism was the solution to the Jews' problem."

"So then," I ask, "did you and my father take the advice
of the harbor pilot to stay out of the foreign wars in the
Middle East, or did you not?

"No we did not. It was impossible to do that if you were
in Aliyah Bet. The Brits damn near made it impossible."

"How so," I ask?

"Well. It's going to take another *alt geshikhta* to explain
that."

"Well, how did the Baltimore harbor pilot even know
about 'Jew' ships with all the shush-shushing that was going
on," I ask?

Herschel takes in a huge breath and lets out a long
exhale. He explains that not only was the Tradewinds
birthed at Baltimore but there were other Aliyah Bet ships
there also, including the President Warfield, an excursion
liner at one time running between Baltimore and Norfolk
across Chesapeake Bay. Originally a luxury liner with 171
first class staterooms, she was a flagship for the Old Bay
Line run by the Baltimore Steam Packet Company for
tourists. After that she saw service during the war in the
hands of the U.S. Navy, becoming the U.S.S. President
Warfield, which was used during the Normandy invasion as
a control center for logistical operations. Every boat leaving
the beachhead at Normandy had to exchange blinker signals

with her.

When she finally returned to Baltimore Harbor, she was sold for scrap but changed ownership three times thereafter. Then she was refitted before she crossed the Atlantic again, this time renamed The Exodus while at sea. By the time the Tradewinds reached Baltimore, the President Warfield, soon to be the Exodus, had already departed on its second trip across the Atlantic, to become an Aliyah Bet ship, and the local press was carrying stories about the participation of Americans in a secret refugee smuggling ring.

"So while the shush-shushing boys kept exhorting us to keep everything on the hush hush, the secret was already out," Herschel moaned. "I don't know," he exclaims. "The Exodus was not well known until Leon Uris wrote about her. Hell, she wasn't even the Exodus while she was in Baltimore. I think maybe the newspapers were just looking for something to write about and they unearthed a few loose-lipped Aliyah Bet sailors who talked about her future as the Exodus. That must have been enough to light the fires under the local newspaper reporters."

. . .

By now the sun is getting low in the sky and it is time for me to begin the drive back home if I'm going to make it home by a decent hour. But I don't want to miss the next story. So I tell Bloom this, and try to make an appointment to come back the next weekend.

"You see," he says? "I meant what I said. If you wanted to hear all these stories, you should have brought your pajamas with you. So why don't you just drive into Mentor now and buy some pajamas and a toothbrush and whatever else you may need. Go ahead, go. Who knows if I'll even still be alive to finish the stories next weekend when you come back. In the meantime, I'll tell Jaida to put on dinner for three. Go now. Go ahead."

So I call my wife and tell her I'm taking his advice. I'll be home sometime tomorrow.

FIFTEEN

*"To go to the synagogue with one's father on the
Passover eve - is there in the world a greater pleasure than
that? What is it worth to be dressed in new clothes from head
to foot, and to show off before one's friends? Then the
prayers themselves - the first Festival evening prayer and
blessing."*

--Sholem Aleichem

When I return from Mentor, Bloom is prepared for his
next story, complete with visual aids. He's got photographs
of the Tradewinds showing her bridge, her aft cabin or "poop
deck," her two stacks and her aluminum masts. All the
windows on the ship are round, constructed as portholes, and
her main deck is cluttered with lifeboats and rubber rafts.
She looks like an old a derelict ship. Her top speed is twelve
knots or roughly 15 miles per hour.

"We set sail for Lisbon," Bloom says. "This is our
shake-down cruise as an Aliyah Bet boat, and the trip across
the Atlantic is no picnic. On the way to Portugal, we hit
rough water at the tail end of a hurricane but the ship
perseveres at 12 knots. We know she's a clunker, but
except for the dying hurricane at the end of our journey, we
encounter no rough seas. The attitudes among the variegated
crew make life very difficult. There are non-Jewish
American Poles, a Black man, an Irish man, salty
professional mariners, rabbis' sons, an ex-Methodist minister,
Navy veterans and green Zionist youth group members from
New York and New Jersey who've never been on a ship.

"Your father and I were of course the oldest. That is so
even though I am 10 years younger than him. The others call

him pops, and they call me Mr. Bourgeois because, to them, I am a middle class incongruous gentleman farmer who isn't tough enough to go to sea. The name-calling doesn't bother us, but the hard boiled attitudes of the handful of veteran sailors toward the tediously idealistic volunteers from the Zionist Youth Movements eventually gets under everyone's skin. The Zionists seem stuffy to the veterans, and the veterans annoy the Zionists with their course language and rough ways.

"The veterans keep playing jokes on the serious minded Zionists: things like telling them the ship would soon be passing the mail buoy from which they can send their letters home, thus causing these kids to stay up all night writing their parents and sweethearts. They also tell youth group members they plan to remove the forecastle head and sell it to make money when they get into port, laughing as they watch these kids run to an officer to rat out their ridiculous scheme. Unaccustomed to the concept of taking orders from the captain and the officers, the youth group members think the ship should be democratically run, but when one of them refuses an order, he is confined under guard.

"When we reach the Azores, we stop briefly. There, we pick up our first passenger, the sexton of a tiny local synagogue who has fled Europe as a refugee and has been watching Aliyah Bet ships put in to the islands. He explains to us that his little-used synagogue was established by Marranos fleeing the Spanish Inquisition in the 16th Century, but now it has fallen into disuse. Having gained an understanding of what Aliyah Bet is, and what its mission is all about, he pleads with us to take him along with us to Palestine. When we continue on to Lisbon, he's aboard.

"In the Azores, four young Haganah members from Palestine also join us. They are to be our ship's officers, our voyage commanders, so to speak, when we sail for Palestine. We take one look at them and we're very skeptical. How do we agree to trust these very young men with our lives?

They're all practically just out of their teens. It also seems that all they want to do is overdo security. Like Danny Schind, they are big on shushing us. Everything has to be a big secret, even though it seems the secret that Americans are participating in Aliyah Bet is already out. Everyone on the islands apparently has expected we would be Americans when we showed up, and there is much talk among the locals about the Americans from other ships who've already been here before. Thus, security gets more and more lax. In fact, we are beginning to let it go altogether, talking openly about our plans to ferry refugees to Palestine.

"We soon learn, however, that our oath to the Haganah is for real, as was our agreement to put ourselves under Haganah's command and discipline. This happens when a number of the younger Americans refuse to stay aboard the ship for security reasons while the Haganah boys are enjoying shore privileges. The Americans who defy these orders are taken ashore and sent to Ponta Delgada where they are subjected to a court-martial, and threatened with being sent home. Ultimately, however, they are allowed to sail on with us to Lisbon

"Waiting for us at the dock in Lisbon is a Palestinian named Yehoshua Baharav, alias Captain Diamond, a kibbutznik with a Canadian passport and a false identity, who is the Haganah's local representative. His cover story is that he's an official of the United Fruit Company, but in reality he has previously commanded one of America's Aliyah Bet ships, the <u>Haganah</u>, and he has aided another boat from the United States, the <u>Haim</u> <u>Arlosoff</u>, in getting out of Sweden with 664 refugees aboard by arranging for their railroad train to take them to Trelleborg Harbor at the last minute, instead of to Sweden's second largest city, Goteborg, where the British are watching to interfere as they embark for Palestine.

"Captain Diamond is renowned for his guile. He has already demonstrated it in dealing with the local authorities in Trelleborg by overcoming their reluctance to allow the unscheduled Haim Arlosoff to sail from there without Swedish authority from above. The delay while waiting for instructions from the naval command in Stockholm could have been fatal if the British had caught on to where the refugees actually were, and from where the Haim Arlosoff was now going to depart.

"Diamond accomplishes his goal by bringing in a Jewish community elder to convince the local Swedes, always careful to show tolerance, that being a ship full of orthodox Jews, the Haim Arlosoff must leave immediately, because the Sabbath is coming. It must leave before sundown or wait until Monday because nobody will be at work in the port on Sunday, including the Swedish harbor pilot. This will throw the ship entirely off schedule. Actually, the passengers of the ship aren't orthodox but consist of over 500 teenaged Jewish girls earlier rescued from Nazi concentration camps by the Swedish Red Cross in accordance with a deal they made with the Gestapo during the war. Diamond would soon show his guile again when an incident occurs that almost prevents the Tradewinds from leaving Lisbon.

"In the meantime, carpenters build sleeping racks on the Tradewinds, which according to Diamond, are to be used to transport bananas—never mind that bananas have to be transported hanging up from their stems, not laying down on their sides. Toilets are also built on the deck out of wooden slats arranged over a trough.

"Passover is celebrated aboard the ship by the crew with a traditional *seder* prepared by its two non-Jewish volunteers, one of whom is a Polish-American ex-merchant-mariner who learned the traditional recipes from working in a Jewish delicatessen in Chicago for many years. He has volunteered for Aliyah Bet because of the many close Jewish friends he has as a former manager of the delicatessen. The third oldest member of the crew, after Hymie and myself, this Polish American is also an adventure seeker who learned to love the sea before being mustered out of the merchant marine for being too wily of a card-player.

"The other non-Jewish *seder* preparer is a Black man named Josiah Jeffers who used to work for an old Jewish liquidator engaged in buying army surplus in Indianapolis. His former job was to oversee the shipment of the surplus goods from whatever venue they were in, to purchasers with whom the liquidator had made arrangements to sell the goods. He said his boss, Sol, who owned the business always told him, 'Josiah, I don't ever want to see any of the goods I purchase here in Indianapolis. If I do, it means we'll have to arrange for their storage, and if that happens, we won't make any money on them.'

"Josiah became very close to Sol. He was always at Sol's house for Jewish holiday dinners, including *seders,* which he loved because they reminded him of "when Israel was in Egypt land" from the negro-spiritual *Go Down Moses.* The problem was Sol was ancient. When he died none of his boys wanted the business. So Josiah was out of a job.

"Once when we were at sea Josiah asks your father, 'Why do you want the Jews to have a home in Palestine? They'd be much better off in America wouldn't they? You're an American aren't you? You know this. And me, a Negro. Look how well we've all done in America after slavery, just staying in the United States and fighting race discrimination and all.'

"I'll never forget Hymie's reply. He says, 'Yes my friend. Do you think you'll ever win? I want Palestine, not for myself, but for the descendants of people in Europe who've lost that battle after 2000 years of suffering discrimination. Six million people they lost, all dead. Their remnant can no longer put up with it, and I have been so lucky to live in Cleveland during their latest defeat. Now getting those who are left to Palestine is the only right thing for me to do. How else can I help repair their world? I don't think President Truman is going to let them into America because, frankly, nobody wants them in America, not in the great masses in which they would come.'"

"While we're in Lisbon, Hymie gets exasperated with all the secrecy we have to maintain about our voyage and about our ultimate goal. From what he saw when we were in the Azores, he knows the big so-called secret of the Jew's American fleet is out, and he greatly misses your mother, whom he felt honor-bound not to tell anything about the Jews' Secret Fleet before he left.

"So he writes her a letter in Yiddish, but he asks me to read it for corrections because he's not a good writer." I tell Bloom I remember seeing a letter with Portuguese postage laying on a table at Ma's house, but I didn't read it because it was in Yiddish and I wouldn't have understood it, even if I could have read the Yiddish words. I ask him if he can remember anything about what the letter said.

"Yes," he replies. "It was very short and plain, almost what a child would write. He told her he was in Lisbon Portugal and not to worry, that he was alright. Without naming our ship or telling her what the Tradewinds was for, he told her that we had celebrated Passover on the ship a few nights ago and that he was missing her.

"He said he couldn't tell her where he was going next, but that he would write her from there when we got there. He also said he had not run into any of his friends or relatives yet, but he expected to see them soon. Where he got that from, I have no idea.

"He asked if your brother was alright—whether there was any more craziness from him, which he hoped not. Oh, then here's the part you'll really want to hear, and I can remember it almost world for word. He said, 'I won't ask if Lazer's alright because I know he is. I'm so proud of him— the way he takes care of his family, and the way he always does the right thing to do. I just hope he and his family are healthy.'

"And that was about it," Bloom concludes. He doesn't notice the tears in my eyes.

"Not everything goes pleasantly in Lisbon as your father's letter from there would suggest," Bloom continues. "In fact, one night the Americans from our ship get into a fist fight over our mission with some British subjects in a bar. Enter Captain Diamond who makes arrangements to pay for all the damage, and who tries to explain the presence of the Tradewinds in Lisbon to the local police. The police are on the lookout for Communists and terrorists, but Captain Diamond tells them the only reason the Tradewinds is in their city is because it's cheaper to refit ships for the banana trade in Portugal. After an investigation, the police are not persuaded, and they place Portuguese guards aboard the Tradewinds and bring in the Portuguese secret police.

"When it's time to leave Portugal, the secret police come aboard to prevent the ship from sailing. Captain Diamond tries to ply them by offering them cigars from the former Portuguese colony of Brazil, and telling them that he's the official of the United Fruit Company in charge of overseeing the refitting of their ships for the banana trade between African countries and Argentina. The police are having none of this, and they demand that he come ashore with them. As the crew watches, there is great tension on board. Nobody can think what to do.

"Knowing that the Palestinian crew members understand Hebrew, Captain Diamond quietly tells them in that language, which the Portuguese cannot understand, to take the ship out of the harbor without a pilot and then to force the Portuguese guards on her into one of her small boats so they can row themselves back to shore. He then leaves the ship and allows himself to be taken into the custody of the secret police.

"But when the crew hurriedly attempts to pull up the anchor it fouls on a metal cable that is mooring the Tradewinds to the dock. Hymie rushes to the engine room to

129

get his tools and then climbs down and stands on the anchor with a hacksaw. The ship leaves only after he painstakingly hacksaws the cable.

"When he comes back on board, volunteers rush around him. 'How did you know to do that,' they ask? 'How did you know what to do?'

'I work with metal,' he says. 'I can fix anything on a ship involving metal. I've sailed on ships before. That's what I told them when I signed up. So I did it.'"

"But I knew, says Bloom, "those weren't the real reasons behind his actions. The real reasons were that your father was afraid of nothing. It seems to me that many times in his life he acted without any understanding or regard of for the possible consequences to himself. This was just another example."

"This must have been one of the old stories the two of you used to sit and jaw about down there in the barn," I say. "You must have laughed about this one a lot."

"It was one of our favorites," Bloom replies. "But let me tell you the rest of the story. When the police chief sees the boat leaving, he confiscates Captain Diamond's passport, and blows his whistle bringing other police running. When they arrive, they attack Captain Diamond on the dock and beat him. Later we learn that he talked his way out of this mess and got his false passport back by telling them his company wanted to send more ships to Lisbon for work, and would do so if only he could get back to his office in France. As the time unemployment in Lisbon was extremely high. They let him go.

"I'm not saying there was any bribe involved, but suffice it to say that later that year, the British owned petroleum company in Portugal suddenly refused to sell fuel to Aliyah Bet ships that stopped there. Captain Diamond was able to solve this problem by calling his 'old friend,' the chief of the secret police, and offering to pay him a fee to take care of the matter.

SIXTEEN

"It is hoped that the red herring of 'refugees' drawn by the Jews over their colonization and expansion programs in Palestine has been to some degree exposed."
-- **British Report on Jewish Propaganda concerning Immigration to Palestine, 317ᵗʰ Airborne Field Security Section, Haifa, Mar. 20, 1947**

The next morning Jaida serves us buttermilk pancakes with fresh Maple Syrup, ripened cantaloupe, blueberries and coffee. Herschel digs in and so do I. He brings some old newspapers to the table with him.

"Well," he says, "guess I'd better get started on the next *alt geshikhta,* or you'll be here for yet another day if you want to hear them all. I've also brought some things for you to look at."

"Yes, please go ahead," I encourage him."

"The Tradewinds sailed on to Bogliasco, on the Italian Riviera, where we picked up over 1000 Holocaust survivors for our journey to Palestine. There, we lie at anchor in a cove, as the passengers sneak out to the ship in rubber rafts. They board on two separate nights. The second night, we move to another secluded anchorage at the mouth of a river and the passengers silently row out to us in small boats, so silently, that it seems like we're watching an old fashioned movie with no sound.

"Against my advice, Hymie writes your mother another letter while we're in Italy. He's very excited, and he wants her to know that he's met a cousin of his younger sister's husband Bori, who will be travelling with him for a while.

He says nothing, however, about our ship, or its destination."

"How did all these survivors know to come to Bogliasco to meet your boat," I ask Bloom.

"That, in itself, is a long story," he answers. There was an underground organization known as *Bricha,* which means 'escape,' organized by Polish Jews who fought as partisans. After a post-war pogrom in Poland, they were convinced there was no future for the Jews in Eastern Europe and they joined with the Haganah and members of the Jewish Brigade of Britain to conduct the largest overland secret and illegal mass movement of refugees out of the communist countries that has ever occurred by smuggling them into seaports on the Mediterranean from which they would try to get to Palestine. Bogliasco was one such port.

"Years later, one of our crew members, Paul Kaye from the Bronx, who'd been a marine engineer in the U.S. Navy during the war, described the embarking refugees we took on in The Jewish Star, his hometown Jewish newspaper." Bloom ruffles through the newspapers he's brought to the table and begins reading from one of them:

> "The whole trip, the whole war, that first time I saw my people was the most impressive part of my life." Kaye recalled. "They were haggard; they had all they owned on their backs. They came up, they each hugged and kissed us and said, 'We are going to Eretz Yisroel. We're going to our home.' They were very happy to get the hell out of Europe."

"The oldest passenger who comes aboard our ship is 78. The youngest is 1 year. The average age is about 35. Here is another newspaper containing an article by I.F. Stone of the New York City newspaper *PM,* who sailed with the Haganah, one of the first American ships to head for Palestine on behalf of Aliyah Bet. It's not about the passengers boarding the Tradewinds at Bogliasco for its first trip to Palestine, but it might as well have been because Stone's descriptions typify our passengers. He writes:

'Among our refugees were five Gentiles who intended to settle in Palestine, four for religious reasons, one for idealistic reasons. Two thirds of the refugees were men . . .

'There were Jews from sixteen different countries on board, including one rather lonely Egyptian Jew who spoke only his native Arabic and a smattering of French . . . There were 585 refugees from Poland. The next largest group, 109, Czechoslovakian Jews, most from Slovakia and Carpatho-Russia. There were 84 immigrants from Holland, all young people . . . There were 59 Jews from Hungary, 51 from Rumania, 44 from Germany. Twenty-four from Lithuania. Twenty were from France, 12 from Belgium, and 11 from Austria. There were six Russian Jews, three Latvians, two Swiss, two Turkish, two Greek . . . Linguistically, the ship was a floating Babel . . .

'Yiddish is a common language most of the Europeans on board can use to converse with each other, but those without Yiddish are out of luck, as was the sole Egyptian.'

"Of the crew, only Hymie, Paul Kaye, and I can speak Yiddish. All of the Palestinian crew members are too young to know the language. They speak only Hebrew and English.

"Conditions aboard the ship for the passengers are horrific. Over 80% become seasick, keeping a sizable number of our crew from the American Zionist youth groups constantly mopping up vomit. In accordance with Aliyah Bet policy, the refugees are kept below decks, taking turns going above in small groups for fresh air and to use the jerry-rigged heads, that is, those that can hold their diarrhea until they get there. Two babies are born on board while we are in

the open sea. There is only one washbasin aboard that can
be used for bathing infants, and it must be used in shifts.

"The political views of our passengers are as varied as
their nationalities. Except for the common purpose, as Paul
Kaye put it, of wanting to 'get the hell out of Europe,'
everyone is going to Palestine for different reasons. Here
again, what I.F. Stone wrote about the passengers on the
Haganah suffices as well to describe our passengers. Of the
Haganah, Stone wrote:

'One hundred and thirty-eight persons on board
had no political affiliation. The rest belonged to 17
different Zionist parties, the largest group being
orthodox. There were 195 members of Agudath
Israel and 90 of Poale Mizrachi (orthodox labor).
Next were 140 Revisionists, from the chauvinistic
right. There were 82 Chalutzim from the Hashomer
Hatzair, a left-wing socialist group which advocates a
bi-nationalist Arab-Jewish Palestine rather than a
Jewish state.
Of the 1015 passengers, 568 were chalutzim who
intended to spend their lives in collective settlements
in Palestine. All of them were socialists of one kind
or another.'

"A little over a week out into the Mediterranean, as we
approach Palestinian territorial waters, a British
reconnaissance plane buzzes us twice and flies off. When he
sees this, a Palestinian officer, now serving as our Haganah
commander, orders us to tear down as much of the ship's
superstructure as we can. He wants to disguise us as
something different than what the British scout plane has
seen. But a day later, two British warships appear and one of
them signals us to stop. Warning shots are fired into the air
by their cannon. It appears we are now going to be in the
position of either defending ourselves, or giving ourselves up

to the British.

"Our Palestinian commander prepares us for what some people have called Aliyah Bet's secondary role, propaganda to sway world opinion toward the Zionist cause and against the British blockade of Jews entering Palestine. He knows there's going to be a confrontation, and his aim is to offer resistance without providing reasons for the killing of anyone. He does not want to provoke British fire. In reality, however, he does not want to just give up.

"Hymie and I work feverishly with the rest of the crew to clear the decks of lifeboats and the davits from which they hang, tying them to the smokestacks. Knowing that the passengers will want to try to defend themselves, the commander orders all fire axes thrown overboard to prevent their use against Britain's sailors if and when they attempt to board us.

"Why has the Haganah thrown all our axes into the sea," Hymie cries out? "Is the commander crazy?"

"He does not want any Brits killed, and he does not want to provoke them to kill us," I yell back. "There is going to be a fight coming."

"The commander then orders Hymie to announce in Yiddish over the public address system that the Haganah wants all passengers to come up on deck. 'We will put up a peaceful resistance to the capture of our ship,' Hymie announces. 'Everyone is to be on deck!'

"The commander next orders the ship's radio operator to break silence and to notify the international press services, Radio Free Europe and the BBC that Haganah ship _"Hatikvah"_ has been ordered by two of Great Britain's Naval ships to heave to in international waters. He says, 'Tell them this is illegal. We are not going to stop.'

"It is at this point that he renames our ship _Hatikvah_ for her likely confrontation with the Royal Navy. As you may, or may not know, Hatikvah is now the Israeli national hymn or anthem. In Hebrew it means 'Hope.' An Irish-American

Catholic crew-member scrambles up one of the stacks and paints a huge Jewish Star on the funnel with the words 'Eretz 1947' under it. Below this reference to the land of Israel, he paints a shamrock and the words 'Eire 1922,' in an attempt to identify the Zionist cause with the earlier Irish Nationalist struggle for independence against Great Britain. It's a truly 'in your face' insulting act for the sailors on the British boats to see.

"One of the British destroyers pulls along-side us. A voice from the British ship yells through a bullhorn, 'Your voyage is illegal; your ship is unseaworthy. In the name of humanity, surrender.'

"When the British destroyer asks that the Hatikvah's captain identify himself, the Haganah Commander brings a boy of 10 years old to the bridge, with a captain's hat on his head, who says in his high-pitched voice, 'I am the captain.' The British destroyer then makes a sharp turn throwing up waves which violently rock the Hatikvah, causing panic among her passengers on deck, who begin running to the other side of the ship. Realizing this may capsize the Hatikvah, the Palestinian commander calls Hymie to the bridge again and tells him to order everyone in Yiddish to sit down, which stops the ship from capsizing. The destroyer then turns around and approaches the Hatikvah in an attempt to board her. She veers away only when I and some other crew members drop a lifeboat davit down from our deck striking her.

"Some time goes by, and two more British ships join the two destroyers assailing us. We next see one of the destroyers coming toward us, making another pass, but this time there are marines on her deck in full battle gear. They fire their rifles into the air. They pull along-side; metal walkways are thrown from their ship to ours; and the marines begin to board us. Canned goods are hurled at them by our crew. Then comes tear gas fired by the British, and hand to hand fighting begins. The British keep firing shots into the air as we fight.

"The next time I see your father, he's angry, standing there in a blood-soaked shirt holding his head where he's received a huge gash. He's on his way to the galley to look for a knife. 'Look at me,' he says. 'The enemy has clubbed me in the head, and the pain, the pain has made me so mad. I want to hit someone, to kill them. What can we accomplish by just throwing cans of food at them? They have guns and tear gas and uniforms, and they have all been trained. I have no training in this. We are going to be captured if we don't do something. Why did they throw the fire axes overboard? I didn't come here for this. I came to take my relatives, my brothers and sisters to Palestine.'

"He tells me he's just come from the engine room where two Haganah officers are working, without success, to rig the ship's rudder and steering mechanism so the boat can be steered from below decks with auxiliary controls. The idea is to destroy the steering mechanism in the wheel house and to lock themselves below, from where they can steer the ship and run it from the engine room when the Tommies succeed in capturing the bridge.

"'You know what I saw when the Haganah officers failed to accomplish this mission with the steering gears,' Hymie yells? 'The commander comes down to my engine room and tells them where to hide when the ship surrenders and is taken by the British to Haifa. When we reach Palestinian territorial waters, he tells them, Ari you go in that tank over there, and don't come out until the Jewish cleaning crew comes aboard in Haifa. Then you can leave disguised as one of them. Tsvi, you hide in that tool closet over there, and do the same thing. Me—he tells nothing. I guess I'm supposed to be on my own. But I know what he's telling them because I have enough Hebrew to understand.'"

"So as one would expect, we fail in our attempt to defend our ship and the British take it over. After the battle of the <u>Hatikvah,</u> she's escorted to Haifa under the control of the British Navy, where six of her American crew are arrested and one goes free by swimming to shore and posing as his brother who is studying at the Technion Institute in Haifa. The representatives of the school fraudulently vouch for him as their student. The rest of the Americans, including Hymie and myself, manage to disappear, posing as refugee passengers.

"Largely, due to Hymie's ability to speak Russian and my Hungarian, we wind up in Cyprus. We simply cast our Aliyah Bet shirts aside; wash the grease and grunge from crewing the ship off our hands; put on caps and clothes like the refugees wear; grab some flimsy suitcases like they have; and, meld in with them. It's all Hymie's idea.

'Use your brain he tells me. Disguise yourself as a refugee if you don't want to be arrested. It's the only thing we can do because we don't have guns and swords like the *goyim* do. So we can't fight them. We weren't trained to fight them. As an uncle of mine once told me, all we Jews have to survive with is our wits.'

"So we simply walk off the boat with the other refugees at Haifa and let ourselves be taken into custody by the British who ship us on a prison ship in large wire cages to Cyprus. Believe me, it's a safer thing to do than hiding in tanks and closets on the ship like our Palestinian crew members. What if the British decide to search the ship and they find these stowaways?

"We stay fourteen weeks on Cyprus at a DP Camp in a place called Xlotympou. 16,000 displaced Jews live in twelve camps on the island. They are camps where the British formerly interned their German prisoners of war. Conditions are very harsh, with poor sanitation, over-crowding, lack of privacy, and a shortage of clean water. We sleep in tents. But despite these conditions, there is a feeling among the Jews that sooner or later we are all going to get to Palestine, either via the British quota system or through other means. Haganah members are very evident everywhere in the camps. Apparently, they have used the same system for leaving other captured ships in Haifa that Hymie suggested we use, when they were unable to hide themselves waiting for the opportunity to leave as part of the Jewish cleaning crews that came aboard.

"And the Brits allow us a lot of freedom while we're on Cyprus. The Jews can organize themselves there, and they do so, with each political organization making its own living arrangements. News broadcasts are also permitted, and they are carried in English, Hebrew, Yiddish and Hungarian, and there is a camp newspaper.

"Instead of dispersing among all of the other refugees, the Americans live in their own little colony. Most of them are also planning to wind up in Palestine, where they intend to live out their lives, maybe even in a new Jewish state. Hymie, on the other hand, is very dejected. So am I. We don't plan to live in Palestine. We both want to go home, as do a handful of other Americans, and we don't know how we're going to get home.

"After fourteen weeks on Cyprus, we are included with some of the other Hatikvah crew members in a shipment of refugees headed for Palestine under the monthly Jewish immigration quota allowed by the British. This has somehow been arranged for by the Haganah. We're scheduled to sail on a prison ship named the Empire Life-guard. But that's a different *Ault Geshikta.*"

"In truth," says Bloom, "as was later reported in The Palestine Post, the refugees, themselves, in their own words, did not offer too much resistance because there were too many children and pregnant women on board. Still, the battle was harrowing."

Bloom shuffles through the newspapers he has with him and says, "Ah, here it is. To give you some idea of the danger, The Palestine Post described the Hatikvah, at her moorings in Haifa after her capture as follows:

139

'Her . . . hull was ripped open in several places where the warships had rammed her.

'As for the condition of the passengers, compared to earlier refugees seen at the port of Haifa, for the most part it was fairly good.

But The Palestine Post goes on to say:

'Ten of the refugees were disembarked on stretchers and will probably be taken to the hospital.

'The rest of the passengers were deported to Cyprus on one of the four prison ships waiting for them.

'"Why did we do this,' Hymie asks me, 'if all these people are now going to be taken to prison in Cyprus? Is it all just some kind of a show?'

"You see? He didn't understand our true mission at first. As the commander had said earlier, the seizure of our ship, in fact the seizure of most Aliyah Bet ships, whether European or American, was virtually inevitable. Extensive British intelligence supported the British blockade of the Palestinian coast, making Jewish emigration to Palestine practically impossible, except under the 1500 per month quota established by Anthony Eden's government. How could we believe the Brits would not learn of each Aliyah Bet endeavor and find us? After all, they had broken the Nazi secret codes at Bletchley Park, their intelligence center, during the war. A multitude of smaller European Aliyah Bet boats had been stopped before America even raised the Jews' Secret Fleet.

"Let me give you a fact as food for thought in answering Hymie's question. Not one of the ten American Aliyah Bet ships ever successfully landed its passengers in Palestine before Israel became an independent state! There was a handful of much smaller European Aliyah Bet ships that had the stealth to successfully complete the voyage before that:

fishing boats, tugs and the like. But not one of the larger American ships succeeded. All of them were intercepted by the British, who either sent their passengers to Cyprus or interned them in the prison camp in Palestine known as Athlit—all except the Exodus.

"Aliyah Bet's first purpose for the American supported Jews' Secret Fleet was to begin taking DPs out of Europe to Palestine, but if that was impossible, its second purpose was to overload the DP camps on Cyprus until Britain had nowhere else to put these Holocaust survivors but to send them to Palestine. The thought was, the British would become afraid they would face a revolt on Cyprus if they didn't let them into Palestine. After all, no other European country would take them, not Britain, not France, not Germany, not Poland, and America wasn't about to take them either.

"When the Exodus, previously named the "President Warfield," was stopped, the British did not even deport its passengers to Cyprus or take them to Athlit from where they could someday perhaps enter Palestine by waiting out the quota system of Anthony Eden's government in London. Rather they were sent back to France, from where they had embarked, and when they refused to disembark there, the Brits expelled them deeper into Europe to Hamburg, which was in the British Zone of occupied Germany. Perhaps that is one of the reasons the Exodus attracted the attention of the writer, Leon Uris. It seemed England was changing its policy. Usually, when captured and boarded, the ships would be interned at Haifa, and either the British prison camp at Athlit in Palestine, or a British DP camp on Cyprus would become the destination of their crews and their passengers. From there, they could eventually become part of the 1500 per month immigration quota, but who knew what would happen to the people from the Exodus who were sent deep back into Europe.

"So it seems that the British generated propaganda

David Selcer

against themselves on their own with the Exodus Affair. It was their idea, not the idea of Aliyah Bet, to send the Exodus passengers back into what was once the heart of Nazi Germany."

.

.

SEVENTEEN

"Barking dogs don't bite, but they themselves don't know it."

Sholem Aleichem

"So now you've got me really confused," I tell Bloom. "You had me convinced my father was a hero, but now I'm wondering if he didn't just foolishly run off and allow himself to be used as a propaganda tool of the Zionists when he wasn't even a Zionist himself. Dad was always capable of making a fool of himself, you know, especially with his mindlessness toward the consequences of his own actions to his personal well-being."

Bloom looks at me askance. From his facial expression, I gather he doesn't like the comment I've made about my father, or maybe it's just my reference to Zionist propaganda. Whatever it is, he looks very disappointed.

"As we sit here in 1975," he says, "with the UN's General Assembly just having passed its 'Zionism is racism' resolution, it sounds to me like you might actually believe the UN's crap and that Zionism was just built on propaganda."

"No," I answer, "I'm simply commenting on my father's penchant for stubbornness, and the situations it got him into. . ."

"Before going on," he interrupts, "perhaps we should examine the attitudes of some of the British at the time. You know Great Britain wasn't just having trouble governing Palestine at the onset of World War Two and thereafter. It was also having big troubles in its largest colony, India. I

143

don't say that to excuse anti-Semitic attitudes of some individual Brits who harbored negative pre-conceptions about Jews. As you know, some Brits can be quite snippy and racist when it comes to their more deeply engrained attitudes of discrimination, and this includes some of Britain's highest government officials.

"But when is anti-Zionism anti-Semitism, and when is it not? One can say the UN's policy today is anti-Semitic, but the British policy back at the time of Aliyah Bet, though harsh, was not born out of systemic political anti-Semitism. For instance, at the end of World War Two, the British Labour Party voted to rescind the White Paper and to establish a Jewish state in Palestine. What could be more pro-Zionist and more pro-Jewish? But in 1946, when President Truman pressed Britain to immediately admit 100,000 Jewish refugees, survivors of the Holocaust who wanted to immigrate to Palestine, British Foreign Secretary, Ernest Bevin goes against the view of his own party, by persisting with the White Paper policy; and, at a Labour Party meeting says, 'There has been agitation in the United States, and particularly in New York, for 100,000 Jews to be put in Palestine. I hope I will not be misunderstood in America if I say that this was proposed by the purest of motives. They did not want too many Jews in New York.'

"Is this an anti-Semitic remark? It is made even after Bevin's own party, has voted to establish a Jewish state. And, after the remark, Bevin goes on to keep the White Paper policy limiting Jewish immigration to Palestine in effect until the British depart Palestine in May 1948.

"But the basic policy of the British government is not one of anti-Semitism during these times, in my opinion. They are simply caught between the practicalities of their reliance on Arab oil; their need for the friendship of the Arabs, as well as the difficulties of governing a state with two separate peoples in it, and the exigencies of their own foreign policy of twenty-five years earlier expressed in the

Balfour Declaration. Many English politicians ardently supported the Jews as a people, Winston Churchill for one, and Lord Josiah Clement Wedgwood for another. Wedgwood was critical of appeasement and of the White Paper's limitations on Jewish migration to Palestine, as well as England's refusal to allow German Jewish refugees into Britain. He worked tirelessly to help European Jews. That is why the first North American Aliyah Bet ship, the Wedgwood, was named after him. Furthermore, between 1900 and 1949, there are 41 Jewish members in Britain's Parliament. Having this many Jews in the Parliament is hardly the action of an anti-Semitic government, or an anti-Semitic electorate for that matter. So what was happening?

"As you know, the Balfour Declaration in November 1917 was a letter from the United Kingdom's Foreign Secretary, Arthur Balfour, to Lord Walter Rothchild, the leader of the British Jewish Community." Bloom thumbs through his papers to find a copy of the document; then goes on to read it. "It stated:

'His Majesty's government view with favour the establishment in Palestine of a national home for the Jewish people, and will use their best endeavours to facilitate the achievement of this object, it being clearly understood that nothing shall be done which may prejudice the civil and religious rights of existing non-Jewish communities in Palestine, or the rights and political status enjoyed by Jews in any other country.'

"The Balfour Declaration demonstrates the first public support of a major political power for Zionism, but its impetus, some say, does not necessarily spring from moral or altruistic concerns for the safety or happiness of the Jewish people. Rather it springs from two interests: 1) the British War Cabinet's tactical concerns over the Allies' progress in the First World War, because the Germans were starting to win on the western front; and, 2) Britain's geo-political interests in destroying the Ottoman Empire. Britain wanted to divide the Ottoman Empire up among the Allies with Great Britain taking control of the Sinai and Palestine. She felt she needed this to protect the Suez Canal in British controlled Egypt for Britain in order to enhance British imperial domination over India, militarily and economically.

"At the time, Germany was turning the tide of the fighting in its favor in France, and the American's had not yet fully entered the war. The British felt the Balfour Declaration, expressing their support for the Jews would appeal to Jews in Germany and particularly America, given that two of Woodrow Wilson's closest advisors were avid Zionists; and, the United Kingdom also hoped to encourage support for Britain's goals in Palestine from the large Russian Jewish population that had suffered pogroms over the years. Thus, they believed support for the Zionist's would hasten America's entry into World War One and reduce Germany's effectiveness by turning her own Jews against her. In addition, they believed the Balfour declaration would help to pre-empt French pressure they expected for an international administration of all the previous Ottoman lands. Perhaps helping Jews get to Palestine could cause the huge Russian Jewish community to side with the Brits against the French goal of limiting Britain's influence in the Middle East.

"Twenty years later, although they had accomplished their goals in World War One and in the Middle East, the British find they have hoisted themselves by their own petard with the Balfour Declaration. The Arabs hate it! They are asking Hitler to prevent its implementation and making noises about becoming his ally in the Middle East.

"But Great Britain needs the Arabs for support to overcome Hitler's invasion of North Africa in World War Two, and they are afraid the Balfour Declaration has turned the Arab world against them. Hence, they back up on the Balfour Declaration by enforcing their White Paper which severely limits the pace of Jewish migration to Palestine. As World War Two ends, the Brits also seek Arab oil and fear Communist Russia's advancement into the Middle East.

"So you need to understand that Britain's 'flip-flop' on Jewish immigration to Palestine did not necessarily occur because of anti-Semitism," Bloom concludes. "Rather, the Brits were simply pursuing their own foreign policy self-interests, as required by the times, as every other nation does. While this may appear unbearably, even immorally, selfish and self-centered, it is different than pursuing a policy of hate for Jews. You see, it's all based on geo-political considerations, not hate.

"But the Brit's new policy is not winning the day for them with the Jews, and various statements made out of frustration from their foreign secretary, Ernest Bevin, make them *look* anti-Semitic. His obduracy reflected not only concern for Arab friendship. Human frustration and bitterness were also factors. Beyond the scores of its personnel killed and wounded in Palestine at the hands of Zionist terrorists there, Britain has been shamed before the world by the dilapidated flotilla of American Jewish refugee vessels, and exposed to the endless diplomatic harassment by U.S. President Harry Truman.

"Bevin ranted that the Jews had successfully organized a worldwide conspiracy against Britain and against him personally; the whole Jewish 'pressure' was a gigantic 'racket' operated from the United States; and, 'the Germans might have learned their worst atrocities from the Jews.'

"Boy, that sure sounds like anti-Semitism to me," I tell Bloom.

"Does it? Or is it merely an example of frustration caused by a fine line between anti-Zionism and anti-Semitism that some people claim exists?"

An insight into Ernest Bevin's rage was provided by

Richard Crossman, a Labour MP, who met with the foreign secretary in August 1947, and was obliged to sit through an anti-Zionist tirade. When Crossman heard Bevin's rant, he concluded from it that Bevin had become insane on the Palestine issue. In actuality, what Bevin had failed to realize was that Jewish nationalism was a real force supported by real people prepared to fight and endure hardship, and that Aliyah Bet wanted nothing more and nothing less than a free Jewish nation in Palestine, so it filled up the camps on Cypress so much that it forced the Brits to open them and send the overcrowded inmates to Palestine.

"Many British civil servants and military officers who weren't 'insane on the Palestine issue' made the same mistake, however. In their cases they were letting their preconceptions about Jews, as people, color the clarity of their thinking. They stereotyped Jews in British administrative documents that they were preparing as conspiratorial and untrustworthy. In March 1947 a Brit named Captain J. Linklater, the Commanding Officer of a British Field Security Section, stated in his report that the people on Aliyah Bet ships were not really refugees, but rather part of 'a deliberate campaign of Jewish propaganda to . . . gain world-wide sympathy for the Zionist cause on entirely bogus humanitarian grounds.' His reports characterize Aliyah Bet as a well-oiled plan for making money by getting certain Jews into Palestine in order to cash in on the development of the country. 'It does not appear, in any way whatsoever, to resemble a plan for saving the starving, ill and crippled masses of Jews in Europe today, and of offering them sanctuary in the Holy Land,' Linklater wrote.

"Now that's real anti-Semitism to my mind. British Naval officers refused to accept at face value the appearance of Aliyah Bet ships when captured, instead arguing that when they embark from Europe their passengers look fat, happy and self-confident, but that orders are given about a

148

day before reaching Palestinian territorial waters to convert
the ships into 'pigsties' with the settlers on board appearing
to be in a wretched state of filth, poorly dressed and
disheveled with anxiety written all over their faces. In the
minds of some British Navy officers, it was all a conspiracy,
a Zionist propaganda ploy to sell their 'refugee' story, and
Zionism itself was a vast propaganda machine at work in
Europe for the purpose of persuading Jews to leave their
homes for the supposed fresh, open air agricultural life
awaiting them in Palestine on collective farms. In other
words, Aliyah Bet passengers had all been brainwashed with
Zionist teachings. Naval officers wrote snide remarks like
this into their reports with no fear that their superiors would
object. *That* was anti-semitism.

"Traditional British fears of Soviet influence also
clouded the views of Captain Linklater and other Brits when
15,000 Jews received permission from Russia to leave Soviet
controlled areas of Eastern Europe for the Middle East on
two American Aliyah Bet ships known as the Pan York, later
named Kibbutz Galuyot (Ingathering) and the Pan Crescent,
later named the Atzmaut (Independence). Captain Linklater
worked hard but unsuccessfully to prove that Jewish
immigrants from Soviet- controlled Eastern Europe were
Communist spies, actually searching many refugees for
communist documents that never turned out to be existent.

"It's against this background that you need to evaluate
whether your father was a hero or just a "tool" used for
propaganda purposes. From 1939 until the Second World
War ended in 1945, Aliyah Bet's efforts had succeeded in
successfully smuggling only 6000 Jews into Palestine with
small boats in the face of Britain's White Paper quota
system. By the end of 1945 Britain had allowed only
another 13,100 Jews into that territory for the entire year
under the quota system. The Jews of Europe had few other
places to go but Palestine when the war ended because
immigration to the United States and Britain was severely

restricted and they were unwelcome in their former homes in Europe. Your father participated in a Zionist plan to fill the camps on Cypress until they burst at the seams, not propaganda.

"As of the end of the war, in addition to the trickle leaving for Australia, South Africa and South America, there were over 100,000 displaced refugees desiring to leave Europe for Palestine. By using the much larger ships of the Jews' Secret Fleet from America, the Haganah succeeded in filling up the prison camp at Athlit in Palestine and the DP camps on Cyprus with thousands of refugees who were seeking new homes in Palestine, a pressure which the now crumbling imperial United Kingdom could neither pay for nor withstand. So it quit Palestine and turned the matter over to the UN. The UN then partitioned Palestine, and opened up the DP camps in Cyprus allowing their inhabitants to go to Palestine.

"We know the rest of the story from there. Today, millions of Jews, born from this remnant of post-war European Jewry, are living in Israel. Your father had a hand in all this, not because he was a Zionist, and not because he was anyone's 'tool,' but because he wanted to help save the original 100,000, and he did. All he really knew was that they had no place else to go and that his family and the family of your mother might be among them. Was he a tool of so-called Zionist propaganda? I think not. Had he shown injudicious regard for his own safety. Yes, that was Hyman Zeltzer."

EIGHTEEN

"British Fight Terrorists in Jerusalem; Holy Land Disorders Follow Deportation of *Warfield's Passengers,"*
Baltimore Sun, July 27, 1947

When Bloom concludes his remarks about my father, we let go of the subject of Aliyah Bet long enough to eat lunch. Jaida brings us wheat crackers with smoked oysters, Kaiser rolls, kosher salami, mustard, herring in cream sauce and a little potato salad. After lunch she insists on taking Herschel out in his wheelchair for a walk and a little fresh air. When she brings him back to the porch, he's ready to tell the next *Ault Geshikhta.*

"As I was telling you before," he says, "after fourteen weeks on Cyprus, we are scheduled in July 1947 to leave with the rest of the Hatikvah's crew in a group of refugees the British have selected to go to Palestine under the British quota system. The Haganah plays a role in seeing that the Hatikvah's crew members are selected for this trip for a very special reason. We are carrying with us all the pieces of a bomb that has been constructed on Cyprus. We are to sail on the British prison ship Empire Lifeguard overnight to Palestine, and the bomb will be used to sink the Empire Lifeguard after we get there.

"This is a new chapter for Hymie and me in our Aliyah Bet adventure: a chapter of pro-active violence against the British. Haganah has ordered the bombing because of something that happened with another American Aliyah Bet vessel, the Exodus, which was captured on July 18, 1947.

151

David Selcer

For the first time in the history of Aliyah Bet, the British attacked an Aliyah Bet ship outside of Palestinian territorial waters, ramming her, killing three Jewish passengers aboard the Exodus and wounding 146 others."

"'I only signed up to take refugees to Palestine,' Hymie protests. 'I don't want any part of bombing British ships.'

"'You also swore an oath to the Haganah when you signed up, and you agreed to put yourself under the orders and the discipline of the Haganah,' a Haganah officer reminds him while we were still on Cyprus.

"'They told me I could go to jail or even lose my life when I volunteered, but they did not tell me I would be bombing anything or anybody,' Hymie continues to argue. But when they tell him that he's either to board the Empire Lifeguard carrying part of the bomb or stay on Cyprus indefinitely, he agrees to comply.

"One of the Haganah Officers responsible for getting us included on the Empire Lifeguard's trip is Leila Halivy, a buxom 38-year-old member of Kibbutz Kfar Giladi. She is a *sabre* who speaks English as well as Hebrew and some Yiddish. Sabras are Jews actually born in Palestine, and she looks every inch a sabre, tight short shorts, muscular thighs, combat boots up to her round calves, a blouse with rolled up sleeves, and long hair tied up in a scarf exposing her high forehead. Married at a young age, she has lost her husband during the 1929 Arab riots in Jerusalem. Joining the Haganah thereafter, she helped crew the Haganah ship, Norsyd/Balboa, the second American manned boat attempting to run the British blockade of Palestine, and the only one to make two such voyages. When the second voyage of the Norsyd/Balboa ended with her capture outside the port of Haifa, Leila is interned at the British prison camp at Athlit in Palestine. From there she's eventually sent to Cyprus.

"In these times it's not unusual for Jewish Palestinian women to develop love interests with outsiders who have

come to help establish the Jewish state in Palestine. Leila is
such a person, and perhaps because of her age, who does she
choose to pursue: Chiam Zelitzer—aka-Hyman Zeltzer?
Why not? He's still a handsome man, even at his age. She
notices him on the first day he appears in Xlotympou at the
detention camp on Cyprus, and she moves on him
immediately.

"'So you're a silver fox,' she tells him. Noticing his
dumbfounded look, she says, 'You know what a silver fox is
don't you? A mature man with silver grey-hair.' Though
accented, her English is quite understandable.

"Having always been self-conscious about his baldness,
Hymie is immediately embarrassed. 'Nobody has ever
called me a silver fox at home,' he stumbles, letting out one
of his all-consuming laughs."

"'Home? And where is home if I may ask,' Leila
pursues."

'Cleveland, Ohio in the United States of America.'

"'Oh, an American,' she marvels. 'You don't sound like
an American.' She is referring to his still heavy Yiddish
accent. 'Are you not going to *Eretz Yisrael* to make a new
home there,' she asks?

"Again, a dumbfounded look emanates from Hymie.
Leila notices his head. 'I see you are wounded,' she says.
'Let me take a look at that. I can help you,' and she reaches
up for his head, grazing her body against his and gently
manipulating his forehead with her thumbs. 'Oh, it's quite a
gash. You need stitches. Come with me.'

"She leads him to a first aid station. Immediately,
Hymie decides they will be friends. Leila comes every day
to the tent where he is staying to check on his head and the
two of them sit and talk. Hymie doesn't realize what's
happening to him, but I do. He's falling for her.

"When we board the Empire Lifeguard, and the
Americans, with their bomb, see that we are all going to be
split up in separate locked wire cages in the belly of the

153

prison ship, there is great concern. These cages are large, but there are many refugees boarding. We Americans must all stay together if we are to accomplish our purpose. Suddenly, we see Leila, already installed in one of the cages. She is being shipped to Palestine too. She calls to Hymie, and she tells the British guards he is her husband and he should be allowed to be with her. She then tells the other women in her cage to call to the other Americans and tell the guards the same thing. They do, and the British agree. In that way we all wind up together in the hold of the Empire Lifeguard.

"Our bomb is made of a gelignite explosive kneaded together with some sort of oily substance. It is stuffed into shaving cream tubes which are used to carry the explosive aboard, man by man. The shaving cream has been removed and the gelignite stuffed into the tubes in its place. Then some shaving cream is stuffed in at the top above the gelignite. When British soldiers squeeze the tubes to check their content, the shaving cream at the top comes out, masking the gelignite and the tubes pass inspection. Once again the leery British are deceived.

"The bomb's detonator is smuggled aboard by a sailor who goes by the name Sonny while on Cyprus. We all used aliases while we were there. Sonny brings the suppository-shaped detonator aboard hidden in his rectum. The only difference being, this suppository is hard, making it very painful for him to walk.

"At the bottom of our cage is a hatch in the floor. Our Haganah ship's officer from the Hatikvah tells us all to start singing an Israeli song as loudly as we can. As we do, he begins breaking open the lock on the hatch-cover in the floor of the cage. Luckily, there's nobody below when the hatch is opened, because if there is, we will have to kill him. The bomb is then assembled, sans the detonator, and placed down the hatch.

"Our plan calls for inserting the detonator two hours

before we're to land in Haifa. The detonator has its own timer, and it's set for a precise hour and minute which should give all of us plenty of time to exit the ship before the bomb goes off. So far, all has gone well. We will commit treason against the United Kingdom and we will escape undetected.

"Then, suddenly, just outside Haifa the ships propeller stops and we drop anchor! All is silent as the time seems to fly by and we nervously look at our watches. 'Maybe you should think about disconnecting the detonator,' our fellow American crew member, Paul Kaye, tells our Haganah officer."

"'I don't know how to do that,' he says. 'They only showed me how to arm the bomb, not how to disarm it.'"

"'So what do we do now,' asks one of the other Americans? 'Notify the British there's a bomb aboard?'"

"'A hell of a lot of good that'll do,' says another. 'They might not be able to get the experts they'll need to disarm it in time, and even if they can get the ship moving again, you know that's a sure road to prison when we get ashore.'

"'Yes,' says our Haganah officer, 'and we'll have lost our chance to blow up the Empire Lifeguard.'"

"'From your mouth to God's ears,' Hymie mutters under his breath. He doesn't want to blow up anybody or anything.

"After what seemed an eternity, but was really only about 10 minutes, the Empire Lifeguard finally raises her anchor and moves into Haifa Harbor. As the last passengers finish disembarking, the bomb explodes and the vessel begins trembling convulsively. Slowly she sinks to the bottom of the harbor. The passengers just keep walking ashore and board busses to Athlit Prison where they are going to be held temporarily before their release into Palestine. The bombers are never caught.

"The Empire Lifeguard is sent to the bottom on July 23, 1947, only five days after the British had towed the Exodus into Haifa following a pitched battle with her crew and passengers in which two refugees and one American crew member were killed. 28 Exodus passengers also had to be taken to the hospital, and 3 British sailors were injured.

"When the Empire Lifeguard goes down, news of the battle on the Exodus is still reverberating in the press and on news services around the world. Not only does the bad publicity sting the British, but their new war at sea with the Haganah costs them a lot. A Jewish owned company in Haifa has to be contracted with to raise the Empire Lifeguard from the bottom of Haifa Harbor.

"British Foreign Secretary Bevin is infuriated, so infuriated that he orders the refugee prisoners taken from the Exodus to be transported on prison ships back to France, from where they started out, instead of to Cyprus, as is normally done. Normally they would be held on Cyprus until an opportunity opens for them to enter Palestine under the limited long and drawn out British quota system.

In France, however, further bad publicity awaits the British. There, the Exodus prisoners refuse to disembark Britain's prison ships at Port de Bouc, and the French government refuses to make them to do so by forcible means. A stalemate arises. The British prison ships containing the refugees remain off shore at Port de Bouc for more than three weeks, while Britain threatens the Jewish Agency that if the refugees continue to refuse to disembark in France, they will be taken even deeper into the heart of Europe.

Finally, Bevins orders them deported to Hamburg in the British sector of Germany, far away from any port from which they might sail to Palestine if another chance arises. But in Germany things, get worse. 2500 British troops are at the ready at Hamburg Harbor with tear gas and clubs. When the refugees on one of the prison ships engage in a sit-down strike, the Brits drag them ashore. On one of the other prison ships, the refugees battle paratroopers and military police for two hours before being removed from the ship. There is a bombing attempt on the third prisoner ship to reach Hamburg that fails.

"The British are angered because of the bombing of the Empire Lifeguard and because of all the bad publicity the Exodus affair has caused them, so angry that they begin imposing a penalty fee on each Aliyah Bet refugee they capture who is thereafter transported to Cyprus. They attempt to make the Jewish Agency pay it. In this way, Bevin attempts to exact punishment of the Zionist cause for its activism.

NINETEEN

"Without love our life is ... a ship without a rudder ...
like a body without a soul."

--Sholem Aleichem

"Surprisingly, however," Bloom opines, "the Brits don't
turn around and ship us back to Cyprus from Athlit as a
punishment for our transgressions on the <u>Empire Lifeguard,</u>
even though they know that someone on our ship associated
with the Haganah had to have been the bomber. Once in
Athlit, we all just stay there, awaiting release. Maybe that's
the catch. Release could take days, or it could take weeks or
months.

"Athlit is a prison camp surrounded by barbed wire and
prison towers established by the British in the late 1930s
about 12 miles south of Haifa for the internment of refugees
attempting to illegally enter Palestine. It is a very stark place
with Spartan dwellings, 80 of them, and with little to do to
occupy one's time. A few months after World War Two
ended in Europe, a special forces unit of the Haganah broke
into the camp and released 200 detainees, who escaped.
Following this event, the British started deporting illegal
immigrants to the Cyprus internment camps.

"Upon arrival at Athlit, the men and the women are
separated and told to strip naked for delousing in the
showers. To Hymie and me, this requirement, while
inconvenient, does not seem that unusual. After all, Athlit is
a detention camp. Disease must be prevented. But we
become alarmed when we hear great screaming arising from
the women's showers, and some of the male refugees we are

with begin pounding ferociously on our shower door.

"'It happens because the showers remind people of the gas chambers in Poland and Germany,' Leila says. 'Don't forget, these people are all Holocaust survivors. To them there's no difference between the British prison guards and Nazi prison guards. It will take them some time to learn to trust. I've seen this before.'

"You've been to Athlit before,' I ask her?"

"'Oh yes,' she answers. 'As I have told you while we were on Cyprus, I was on one of your American boats, the Norsyd/Balboa, as a Haganah Officer, when the ship was captured by the British during its second run to Palestine. The British took us all, refugees and crew alike, and imprisoned us in Athlit before they sent us on to Cyprus. During my last visit here, there was almost a riot with the delousing procedure because it reminded the refugees so much of what the Nazis did in the concentration camps. Only when they realized they weren't going to be gassed did the riot stop.'

"'How long has this camp been open,' Hymie asks?

"'Since 1938, when the White Paper was issued. It was closed in 1941 around the beginning of World War Two because the British had their hands full with other things then, and it was reopened when the war ended in 1945, as the Holocaust survivors began attempting to come to Palestine. Come. Let me show you something,' Leila says. She takes us to one of the many rough huts in the camp. Inside this one, scratched into its walls are the names in Yiddish of hundreds of illegal immigrants. Hymie begins reading from the top right hand corner of one of the walls. Then he places his hand over one of the names and stops. 'What is it Chaim,' Leila asks?

"He takes his hand away, uncovering the names. 'This, I think,' he says, 'is my wife's father. They look at the name together scratched in Yiddish:

David Selcer

Rebbe Israel Fogel – Stanislawow – Galicia – 1938

'Think of it Chaim,' says Leila. 'If that's truly him, he was somewhere around the age you are now when he was interned here in 1938.' She grasps his hand. 'Just think of it Chaim.' She leads him out of the dilapidated hut into the sun. 'And now, here you are in Palestine too.'

"Hymie looks off into the distance. What he is thinking I cannot tell. He seems very contemplative. 'It's only nine years, the difference in our age. Maybe you're right. Maybe he's still alive, somewhere here in Palestine. If only I could find him. It would make my Hanna Golda so happy.'

'Maybe you should stay here Chiam and see if you can find him.'

"I don't know why," Bloom continues, "but from that day forward it was clear to me that Leila had personal designs on your unsuspecting father, and she had every intention of pursuing them. She didn't seem to care that he had a wife back in the United States.

"One day, she asks him, 'Have you ever seen a kibbutz?'"

'No,' replies Hymie.

'Then when we get out of here you must come see Kfar Giladi. It is where I live. I will take you there and you can see how you like it. Maybe you will decide to stay awhile.'

'Oh no, I wouldn't want to be a burden on your family.'

"She laughs at him, throwing back her head. Her thick curly red hair settles like a mop of corkscrews on her shoulders. She's 38, but she's in such good condition that she looks 30. And her affect is also that of a younger woman. 'Do you know what is a kibbutz Chaim,' she asks?

'Yes, a collective farm.'

'That is so, but it is more. The kibbutznikim, everyone who lives on the kibbutz, are my family. We don't have families there like the ones you think of. Come with me. You'll see. I'm sure you've never seen anything like it

160

before.'

"Go ahead with her, I tell him. Take a look at where she lives. You might as well be a tourist as long as you're here. I don't know what possessed me to tell him to go. It's almost as if, with all the travails we'd been through on the sea and in the camps, I'd forgotten about his wife, your mother back here, at home in Ohio. I don't know. Maybe I just want to vicariously experience a Palestinian Jewish woman, a sabre myself, through Hymie. I remember, I made him swear to remember everything he saw, and to tell me about it when he got back.

"In the meantime," I tell him, "I'll look into how we can get out of Palestine. We'll need papers and travel documents. It won't be an easy thing to leave because we're Americans. I'm sure the British are going to ask a lot of questions and they are not going to cooperate.

"'No, no,' says Hymie. 'I'd better stay here and help you.'

"Go, go, I tell him exuberantly. I don't want you to miss this because it will mean I'll miss your telling me all about it. Meet me back here in Haifa at the base of the main stairs going up to the Shrine of the Bab on August 1 at 3:00 p.m. You know, the Shrine of the Bab? It's that big white Bahai Temple up there on the hill overlooking Haifa.

"So Hymie and Leila take an *Egged* bus to Metula in the Northern Galilee. Originally an old Druze village which was later settled by Jewish *Moshavim* (farmers) in 1896, Metula eventually devolved from the control of France into British hands in the early 1920s. Leila's home, Kfar Giladi, is south of Metula, but not far from the Lebanese border. It's almost the furthest north you can go in Mandatory Palestine. A jeep from Kfar Giladi picks them up in Metula and transports them to the kibbutz over a bumpy dirt road. The terrain is rocky but beautiful with ample water. It is the site of the ancient city of Dan, which was one of the original Twelve Tribes of Israel. Now, here is what I can remember of what your father told me when he got back from his trip to the north with Leila.

"'So Hymie,' she asks as they're on the last leg of their journey. 'Do you have children?'

'Yes, two,' he answers. 'One is a professional violist, and the other is an accountant.'

'I have one,' she says. 'Eliahu. He's almost 5 years old.'

'But I thought you said you lost your husband years ago. Have you remarried?'

'Yes, I lost my husband years ago. No, I haven't remarried.'

'But . . .

'Shh, Hymie, you don't know what communal living is, but that's what we do. Eliahu lives with all of the other children of the kibbutz in the children's quarters.'

' . . . How do you have a son if you didn't remarry?'

"She places her hands on her hips resolutely and tightens her lips, giving him a very strange, questioning look. Suddenly, as they round a bend, Kibbutz Giladi appears at the top of a small rise in the distance. Hymie can see a blue Jewish Star on the white flag flying over the gate tower of the kibbutz.

'And you and his father? Do you live together? Where does the father live?'

'Shh, Hymie just wait. Be patient. You'll see.'

"When they arrive at Kfar Giladi, at least thirty people come to the gate to greet Leila. One man, Eitan Dahan, is particularly exuberant to see her. On his shoulders he carries a small boy named Eliahu. Leila kisses Eitan and takes the boy in her arms, smiling into his face and chattering at him in Hebrew. Hymie follows as the two of them walk off to Leila's quarters with Eitan. There, they sit with Eitan, and the four of them have tea together. Leila tells Eitan all about Hymie's exploits as a seaman and then as a refugee on Cyprus. It's all in Hebrew. Eitan speaks no English or

Yiddish. So Hymie understands only a little of what she's saying. Eitan, however, seems very impressed. More than once, he reaches out to shake Hymie's hand. He looks into Hymie's eyes expressing his thanks. *Toda Toda! (Thank you)*

"'Eitan is the father of Eliahu,' Leila says proudly. 'He has kept him and cared for him while I am gone, and now that I am back, we can share him again.'

"Hymie looks around Leila's quarters, noticing there is only one single bed and a child's cot. 'Does Eitan also live here.' He asks?

"'Oh no.' she answers 'Eitan stays with Eliahu's aunt, my sister.' Hymie is nonplussed. He averts his eyes from Leila momentarily. She just laughs. 'No,' she says. 'Eliahu is not my nephew. He's my son.'

"Later Hymie learns what early Twentieth Century kibbutz living really is. 'Kfar Giladi,' Leila tells him, 'is a socialist kibbutz, not a religious kibbutz. Everything is shared, and the principle of equality is taken extremely seriously here. The Kibbutzniks do not individually own tools, or even clothing. If a member receives a gift in services—like a visit to a relative or a trip abroad paid for by a parent, there are arguments at members' meetings over it. Is it proper to accept the gift? Should the value of the gift be turned over to the common treasury? Members eat their meals together in the communal dining hall. It's a communal life. And the children stay in communal kindergartens. In some, even many, cases it is not quite clear who their fathers are. They are just shared like everything else.'

"'When the first children were born at this kibbutz.' Leila tells Chaim, 'there were ethical dilemmas that needed to be solved. If the kibbutz was striving for equality, including the equality of the sexes, how could women be seen as automatically being tied to domestic life and child care? Shouldn't these also be the tasks of men? Was it not true that women are only seen as separate because they give birth to children, and was this separation correct and fair? For woman to be liberated and to promote gender equality, they could not be tied to solely domestic duties and child rearing. Kfar Giladi wanted to give women the opportunity to continue their work in the agricultural sector and in the industrial sector. As such, communal education in these areas was the first step towards woman's liberation. Communal child rearing was the next step.'

"'Here, we share everything,' Leila announces proudly."

'Even sexual partners,' Hymie asks?'

'No. by that I mean, everybody gets the same salary. Everybody gets the same healthcare. Everybody has the same type of living quarters, all modest but very pretty. We share all the jobs, from planting to working in the dining room and the nursery to mucking out horse stalls. It is not encouraged, but if, on occasion, there is sex between unmarried consenting adults, or adults who are married to others, nobody has the right to pass judgment.'

'And what if someone's spouse is offended by this?'

Leila explains, 'That is a personal matter to be worked out among the parties involved, and as long as there is no violence or the threat of it, the kibbutz does not get involved.'

'And what if someone refuses to do a job,' Hymie asks?

'We have a council that meets to take care of that.'

'And if someone feels he is not getting his or her fare share?'

'We have a council that meets to take care of that too.'

'And if somebody gets really sick and has to go to the hospital, but the kibbutz is having a bad year economically, how does that get paid for?'

'The Jewish Agency pays for it.'

'So you are a communal society where everything belongs to everybody, including your debts. But what happens if you can't meet your debts?'

'So far, that hasn't happened with any kibbutz that I

know of.'

'But what if it does happen?'

'Then, I suppose we will have to sell our tractors, sell our farm equipment, sell our buildings and our livestock, and move. There, does that answer your question,' she said, obviously peeved?'

"As Hymie explained this conversation to me later, he began to laugh, and it was his big laugh that came out. He was obviously proud of himself. 'For the first time,' he told me, 'I had won an argument using my brainpower over a woman. I was right and she was wrong, and she knew it. For some reason, it made me really like her.'

"Apparently, Leila didn't care about Hymie's little victory. To her it was pyrrhic. She could see that over-all, she was winning in her pursuit of him. He really liked her."

'Want to go for a tractor ride,' she asked? 'I can give you the best tractor ride of your life!'

"'I've never been on a tractor ride,' he tells her."

"'Let me just take Eitan back to the kindergarten and we'll go.'

"On the tractor, she takes him all around the kibbutz, showing him orchards, fields of cattle, chicken coops and chicken yards, grapevines, fields of watermelon, whole fields of flowers, orange trees, fields of wheat and guard towers. She shows him the dining hall, the communal shower, the council meeting room, the livestock barns and the horse coral. She takes him by the rows of living quarters provided to the all kibbutznikim, each with a lovely pergola shading the front door. He marvels at the beauty of the purple wisteria entwined around the pergolas and running from each to each.

"'But where is the synagogue,' he asks?

"'There is none,' she replies.'

"To explain, she embarks on a short description of the Kibbutz movement to him. 'There are many Kibbutz movements in Palestine,' she says. 'Kfar Giladi is a part of the Kibbutz movement associated with *Hashomere Hat*rzair, a socialist-zionist movement, and the Marxist-Zionist political party Mapam. It was founded on 1 April 1927. Artzi kibbutzim, such as ours are more devoted to gender equality than other kibbutzim. Women call their husbands *ishi* ("my man") rather than the customary Hebrew word for husband *ba'ali* ("my master"). There is no division of labor between males and females. The children sleep in children's houses and visit their parents only a few hours a day. The mother and the father share equally in the raising of a child, just as they do in the duties necessary to run the Kibbutz.   Artzi Kibbutznikim are secular, not religious.

'Most mainstream kibbutznikim disdain Orthodox Judaism. Here at Kfar Giladi, we go even further. Many of us are proud athiests, but we still want our community to have Jewish characteristics. The Shabbat is still celebrated on Friday nights with special tablecloths, wine, candles, and fine food, and work is not done on Saturday if it can be avoided. The day of atonement, Yom Kippur, is the day we all discuss our fears for the future of the kibbutz. We also have Bar and Bat Mitzvahs for our children here, once a year, but they are always collective.

'We do not pray three times a day, as do the Orthodox, but we mark holidays like *Shavuot, Sukkot, Passover* with dances, meals, and celebrations. We have also revived *Tu Bishvat,* the "birthday of the trees", as a holiday. This is done because these are all holidays having something to do with farming and growing things, especially Passover and Sukkot, and, of course we see Passover as a national mythical story having to do with our independence.

'Yes, you could say we are all socialists to the extent we seek a utopian collective existence. But we govern ourselves internally through the democratic process. Our kibbutz is also one of the many, that although located where farming is most likely to be productive, is further strategically located for protection against the Arab anti-settlement movements.

You can see the guard towers and fencing in the areas strategic to our defense.

'There is also a Religious Kibbutzim Movement. Since around 1935, these kibbutzim have been established by Orthodox Jews. The orthodox settle in blocks of religious communities for the protection of both their land and their orthodoxy in a secular world. They have also settled in blocks due to their need for joint religious schooling for their children. Most of these communities are around Hebron, the Western Negev and Beit Shean, which is an old cross-roads on the trade route between Egypt and Assyria. Another ultra-orthodox movement, Poalie Agudat Yisrael, has been established by Polish trade unionists who existed between World War One and World War Two.'

"As dusk begins to descend, they find themselves approaching the main yard of the kibbutz, which is the lawn in front of the dining hall. In front of the hall, someone is starting a bond fire, and people are approaching from every direction. The people take their seats in a semi-circle on the grass as an elected leader of the kibbutz begins to speak. 'He is announcing that the children are going to put on a short play about the Jewish holiday of *Shavuot* before the dining room opens for supper. After the play there will be dancing. Do you know *Shavuot?*'

'Yes, it's about the giving of the law on Mount Sinai,' Chaim says as he dismounts the tractor. 'It's also the time of the wheat harvest in ancient Israel. And, it also marks the last day of the Counting of the Omer, which is the seven weeks between Passover and Shavuot when we received the Torah.

'And how do you know all this, Chaim?'

'From *Cheder.* You see the counting of the days and weeks of the Omer expresses anticipation and desire . . .

'Yes, yes, I can see you're a real Torah scholar.' She smiles, pressing close to him and taking his hand.

'But let me ask you something, Chaim
Do you know how to dance the Hora,' she asks?
'No'
'Here, then, I will show you, because we all will soon be doing it. Cross your arms at the wrists.' She does the same, and then takes his hands. 'Now, with your left foot, take a step to the left; cross your right leg behind your left; then another step to the left with your left leg. Then kick your right leg up and skip on your left leg, and then place your right behind your left, and do the whole thing again. Keep doing it as we spin around. There! You've got it!' She laughs. 'Now the only difference when we do it with the group will be that you'll lock your armpits on both sides over the people next to you, and you will spin as the entire circle spins.'

"Hymie watches Leila kick her brown well-formed leg into the air and they turn round and round together in a tight circle. He is apprehensive about how he will do at this dance.

"After the play, he and Leila join the circle that is forming around the fire, and everyone starts moving to the left, around and around, and singing:

Dovid—melech yisrael—chai, chai vikkiom—

"They go faster and faster until he and Leila are both out of breath. Leila is smiling and Chaim is letting go with his hearty laughs until he falls down off his heels. She pulls him back up, now laughing herself, puts her face very close to his, and tells him, 'After we eat, I'll teach you how to do Artza Oleynu. It's the dance of our kibbutz movement.'"

"Eitan joins them in the dining hall. 'You know the Hora,' he says to Chaim? Where did you learn?' Chaim and Leila look at each other and laugh.

"After eating, they dance until the fire turns to embers,

and it is time to go to sleep. One by one the kibbutzniks are falling away toward their rooms to go to bed. 'Where will I sleep,' Chaim asks? 'Is there a guest room on the kibbutz?'

'Yes there is,' Leila answers. 'Your guest room is in my room. I have a Japanese couch. It turns into a bed. Don't worry. You will be comfortable.'

Suddenly, I'm squeamish. I tell Bloom that I don't think I want to hear the next alt geshikhta. It sounds like it may be leading where I don't want it to go.

"Nonsense" he replies! "You came here to learn about your father, didn't you? Who he was and what he did. You must hear the next story. I remember everything he told me about his stay at Kibbutz Giladi. He was very specific about it all."

"I really don't want to hear it," I answer.

TWENTY

"I mention her name and the old pain returns. Forget her, you say? How can you forget a living human being?"
Sholem Aleichem

Bloom continues anyways. "According to Hymie, the next morning is much colder than it has been," he says. "It's a grey dawn and the sun is barely able to burn the dew off the grass. There's a chill in Leila's room. Hymie sleeps soundly. He doesn't hear a rooster crowing outside until Leila's warm touch begins to wake him.

"She has moved from her bed to the futon where he lies sprawled with his head on a pillow over one arm and his feet hanging over the other. She kneels on the floor beside him with her warm hand under his hip. As his eyes open, he sees her healthy looking face, fringed in red curls. Her eyes are deep blue, and he notices her freckles for the first time. He turns on his side to face her putting his back against the back of the couch.

"She smiles warmly and scoots up her warm behind half onto the couch against his lap. He sees her brown round knees with inviting thighs behind them extending from the open slit in her robe, and he can't help himself. He touches them with his free hand, straining upward as he rises off his back. She cups her hand over his and leans her face up toward his.

'Did you enjoy yourself last night, Chaim the Hora man,' she asks?

"Their lips meet, and the dance he was envisioning in his dream before being awakened begins in reality. She roles

170

her body against him, swinging her right leg over to saddle him, locking him into a total embrace. He hugs her, losing his face in her breasts and begins to grind. She opens his shirt tearing at the buttons. The sensation is too much for him and he starts to thrust upward, breathing heavily. She moans as he begins to penetrate, and she cries out in Hebrew. *Al tofsyk!* But he does stop. He has to stop.

"Bloom, I don't want to hear any more of this," I say. "This is not something for a son to hear about his father."

But Bloom continues. "Her shriek ends it all. Momentarily stunned, he loses his tumescence. Confused and ashamed, almost frightened, he's not certain what has happened as he shrinks back on the couch. All he knows is that it's over. His interest wanes. Why can't he . . . His wife, his family . . . guilt?

"How do you know this is what happened," I demand?

"Because he related it all to me in great detail, step by step. I don't know whether he was ashamed of himself, proud of himself, in love with the woman or just confused."

"Still, I don't want to hear it," I say.

"Yes you do. You need to hear it all."

"But, I . . .

Bloom continues talking over my protest. "Suddenly, from outside, an alarm siren goes off, its whirring blotting out thoughts of anything else. 'We're under attack Chaim,' Leila yells. 'The kibbutz is under attack! Quickly, there's a sten gun with magazines and a sleeve in the closet. Get them and follow me! I will get the other one and my pistol.'

"He pulls on his pants and a shirt. She steps into her shorts, wriggles into a sweater and puts on her sandals. They run out the door, Leila in the lead, toward an embankment near the gate. Hyman can see the wire fence atop the embankment, behind which are men shooting rifles, whooping and yelling. A line of bullets from above churns up the ground heading their way, as they both take cover under a tractor. They're on their bellies now, peering around

171

the machine's large driver wheels. 'There's one in the tower by the gate,' Leila screams. She gets up off the ground on one knee and sweeps the tower with her sten gun until a man wearing a red and white checkered keffiyeh falls from the tower. Another Arab peers out from the tower holding binoculars and points down at her, as a third pops his head up, aiming his rifle at her, but Hymie takes them both out with a hail of bullets from his sten before the Arabs can fire.

"Then, as he tells the story, he yells to Leila, 'I got them! I got them for you!' He actually felt pride, he says, that he defended her—like a man. According to him, she yells back '*Ken, todah lecha ohave shli,*' which means, 'Yes thank you my beloved' in Hebrew.'

"But their exchange is suddenly ended when an explosion blows the gates to the kibbutz off their hinges, and thirty or forty men come charging in, firing as they run. From behind Leila and Hymie, bullets are flying over their heads as the kibbutzniks return the Arab fire. Leila and Hymie are caught in a cross-fire. Bodies begin falling around them. 'Just keep your head down Chaim,' Leila yells 'until the Arabs have passed us. Then, we will shoot at them from behind.'

'But there are many more of them outside the gates,' Chaim says. 'Look!' He raises his head to point.

"'Chaim, get down!' She orders him. They both bury their heads in the weeds under the tractor as if they are dead. The body of a shot Arab falls over the back of Hymie's legs. 'Don't move Chaim. Don't move,' Leila commands. She puts her pistol to the man's head and shoots him."

"The dinner bell outside the dining hall starts ringing, and there's a horrific blast from behind. A harsh shrieking sound whistles overhead as a projectile streaks though the air dropping pieces as it goes, until it smashes into the ground beyond the open gates and blows up creating a huge cloud of dust and dirt. 'What was that?' Chaim cries out! 'It was our *Davidka*,' Leila answers, 'Our home made mortar. They ring the bell whenever they shoot it to warn everybody to take cover. Our *Davidka* is notoriously inaccurate. It can kill us just as easily as the enemy, but at least it's loud and it scares the Arabs.' Just then another mortar shot goes off with a tremendously loud crash. The projectile smashes into a cluster of attackers beyond the gate, spewing bodies and blood into the air. Their comrades turn tail and begin running away. A third *Davidka* blast finishes off the threat from outside the gates, but hand-to-hand combat is raging inside on the lawn.

"Leila gets up and begins firing with her pistol. Afraid he'll hit his fellow Jews if he begins shooting his automatic weapon, Hymie throws his sten gun to the ground and joins in the fray with his bare hands, wrestling an attacker up against the wall of the dining hall. The attacker has a pistol in one hand and a knife in the other. Watching the fracas, Leila fires her handgun at Chaim's attacker, but she's out of bullets. Seizing the opportunity, the Arab unloads three rounds from his pistol into her chest, which quickly becomes a bloody mass. She falls. Chaim sees her go down from the corner of his eye and cries out for her. Then he smashes the Arab to the ground and breaks his arm.

"'I turn toward Leila,' he says. 'She's bleeding profusely from the chest and mouth. I cover her with my body, trying to spread over her like a bear rug to shield her from any more harm. All the while I'm crying, telling her, 'I'm here. I'm here. Stay with me.' Suddenly, Eitan appears. When he sees what's happened, he calls one of the kibbutzniks who is acting as a medic. I role off Leila onto the ground next to her, watching her go into shock.'

"As Hymie tells it, the medic picks Leila up from underneath her shoulders, and Eitan grabs her by the heels. They take her to slap-dash clinic inside the dining hall. There, she dies. Eitan is shouting in Hebrew, *'Leila, Leila, Davar iti!* But she says nothing.

"Outside, the battle of the inner kibbutz rages on. Druze

horsemen run through the kibbutz lawn slaying the attacking Arabs with swords from horseback until the Arabs pull back. 'The Druze have always been allies of the kibbutzniks of Kfar Giladi,' the medic yells. 'Many times they have come to our aid like this.' But Chaim is impervious to the battle outside the clinic. He is crying, wailing, over the loss of Leila. Eitan is stoic.

"Lamah? (Why?), ' Chaim asks, struggling with the little Hebrew he knows. Eitan responds in Hebrew, but it's more than Chaim can translate. The blank look on Chaim's face indicates that he doesn't understand Eitan's response. The medic jumps in with English to help him.

'My friend,' he tells Chaim, 'he is saying this is the life of a pioneer for Zionism. Some are lost so that many may go on.'

'Yes,' says Chaim, 'but why were we attacked?'

"The medic translates Chaim's English to Hebrew for Eitan, and Eitan responds in Hebrew, which the medic translates for Chaim."

"'He says it's because they feel this land should be their land, not ours'

'And what do we say to that,' Chaim asks?

'The answer is very complicated,' the medic replies.

"This statement leaves your father cold, as he described it to me later when he returns to Haifa. 'Eitan was a man willing to see his child orphaned, and his one-time lover killed, all because of a *"complicated"* situation? I don't get it! Eliahu was a sabre. Leila was a sabre, both born in Palestine. Eitan was not. He was born in France but came to Palestine as a young child with his family, long before the Nazis came to France. Why? What is the meaning of all this? Why was Eitan brought to Palestine? Was he a pioneer,' Hymie asks, throwing up his hands?

'No,' he answers himself. 'A pioneer is someone who is among the first to explore or settle a new country. Palestine was not a new country. There were already many people,

Arabs, Druze, Bedouins, living there when he comes to
Palestine, and these people are living there a long time.
True, they were living there with some Jews among them,
but the Arabs were in the clear majority. Eitan and his
family didn't have to leave France. They could have stayed
in France many years of his youth before the Nazis came
there? Eitan was not a war refugee like the people we are
bringing to Palestine on the ships. He could have stayed in
France before World War Two. And, he could have gone
back to France and lived there with his family after World
War Two.'

"Could you have stayed in Russia before Hitler sent his
armies there," I asked your father?

"'That is different,' he protests. 'France is tolerant of its
Jews. In Russia we were always having *pogroms*. It was not
as if Eitan was being persecuted and had nowhere else to go
but Kfar Giladi. And, the answer to your question is yes,
even with the pogroms, I probably could have stayed in
Russia, had Hitler never lived, and had my father not thought
up a way of getting me out. Russia was home to millions of
Jews before Hitler. Millions still live there. It was not as if I
had nowhere else to live but Palestine, as was the situation
with the passengers on the <u>Tradewinds</u>.'

"Hymie was very confused when he came back to Haifa
from Kfar Giladi. It was almost as if he was suffering from a
syndrome that it later became fashionable to call 'battle
fatigue.' He simply did not seem to care anymore about the
things he used to care about. He couldn't sleep. He was
listless and often cried. He would not discuss his feelings
about Leila, except to tell me what happened on the morning
of the battle at the kibbutz. It was almost as if he was in
shock. There was no consoling him.

"'You know I killed two people at Kfar Giladi,' he
would say over and over again. I shot my gun at them and I
saw them fall from the tower at the gate, into the brush, two
Arabs. I never knew their names. Who knows if they had

175

wives. Who knows how many children they had.'"

"Yes, Hymie," I would say, "but you had to do it. It was those Arabs or Leila and you."

"'And now, look, Leila is dead too, so what does it matter that I killed these men? Have you ever killed anyone Herschel? Do you know what war is like?

"I look at him silently."

"'Well, I have! I have been in two battles, and I have killed. And, now I am damned," he says!

"His last act at Kfar Giladi was to say the *kaddish* for Leila at her funeral. He thought about taking Eliahu home with him to the United States and there adopting him, but the reality of having your mother, Anne, as his wife for the past thirty years and the existence of his original family quickly intervened. Thank God! You all meant so much to him. So did his time with Leila. I don't think he ever got over that completely—I mean everything that happened that day at Kfar Giladi when the Arabs attacked."

TWENTY-ONE

*"You see how it is, my dear friends. There's no
pleasing everyone. It's hopeless to even try, and the more
you play the peacemaker, the less peaceful things
become."*

Sholem Aleichem

"Hymie came back to Haifa to meet me at the time and
place we had agreed upon: The Shrine of the Bab on August
1, 1947 at 3:00 p.m. He was not happy. He wanted to leave
Palestine immediately, as if his departure could erase his
memory of what had happened at Kfar Giladi. But
something was coming to a head in the country that would
make it very hard to get out of the Middle East just then. It
was the Jewish insurrection against the British. The Arab
conflict with the Palestinian Jews was also boiling
everywhere. There was something very foreboding in the
air: a civil war.

"In the two years since the fighting in Europe had
stopped, Britain's law enforcement forces had lost 103
soldiers, and sustained 391 wounded, because of *Jewish*
militants. It was no longer just the Arabs who were out of
hand. On 15 August 1947, the Haganah blew up the house
of the Abu Laban family, prosperous Arab Palestinian
orange growers, near Petah Tikvah. The Laban farm was
suspected of being an Arab terrorist headquarters. Twelve
occupants, including a woman and six children, were killed.
It was only the beginning of Jewish retaliation against
Arabs. Fourteen months earlier "The Night of the Bridges,"
a Haganah venture in June 1946, occurred in which eleven

177

bridges linking Palestine to the neighboring countries of Lebanon, Syria, Transjordan, and Egypt were simultaneously blown up , in order to suspend the transportation routes used by the British Army. The Haganah knew the British would quickly rebuild the bridges, but their continued disuse was not the point. The point was that the Haganah had shown the British it could co-ordinate an operation as large as the Night of the Bridges to simultaneously damage all the bridges at once. Around the same time various trains were dynamited as they traversed their routes. Two months after that, militant Jewish forces bombed the seat the British administrative headquarters for Palestine at the King David Hotel in Jerusalem. A Jewish insurgency was afoot in the country. Britain began looking for a way to quit Palestine with its honor intact.

"After November 1947, the dynamiting of Arab houses formed a key component of most Haganah retaliatory strikes. Later, on 29 November, the General Assembly of the United Nations voted in favor of recommending the adoption and implementation of a partition plan for Palestine dividing it into Jewish and Arab sections. The resolution had the support of all the big global powers, Russia, France, China, and the United States, but not the support of Britain or any of the Arab States.

"It had become obvious that soon there was going to be a war in Palestine. The question was, would it be a war with the British, or was there going to be war between the Arabs and the Jews. Suffering as he was, Hymie wanted to get out of the area before the war started, to go home to his family in America. We argued vociferously about it, literally yelling at each other.

"I was more open to staying. It wasn't that your father was afraid. It also wasn't simply that we had accomplished our purpose, to get the DPs out of Europe to Palestine. That's what Hymie wanted to believe, but we hadn't. They had all wound up in Cyprus, not Palestine. Hymie knew this and it frustrated him greatly. What was it then? What was Hymie's point?

"As he put it, 'This was just not our war. We are Americans.'

"'Well if it's not our war,' I argued, 'for God's sake then, whose war is it? Why did we work so hard to bring displaced persons from Europe to Palestine if we weren't willing to stay and fight for their right to live here? Of course we're American first, and we're Jews second. But the entire world doesn't work the way America does.'

"Many of the Americans who manned the 'Secret Fleet of the Jews,' in fact, did stay and fight in Israel's war for independence. But Hymie saw it differently.

"'You want to stay because you believe in a cause,' Hymie argued. 'Zionism, a Jewish nation with a Jewish national home. This is a feeling you have inside yourself, and you're beholden to it. But I don't believe in idealistic causes. I believe only in doing what is necessary if it's the right thing to do. It was necessary to help get people, maybe my own relatives, out of Europe after Hitler's war, and it was the right thing to do because nobody wanted them back in their original homes—not in Poland, not in Ukraine, not in Germany, nor in Austria or Hungary—and the doors to immigration everywhere else were closed. Palestine was the only place they had to go.

'So I did what was necessary and right. I helped get them to Palestine. But now the situation has gotten *complicated* according to what I learned up at Kfar Giladi. In fact, I first learned the English word *complicated* at Kfar Giladi. Apparently, it means a lot of things in this part of the world, like the Arabs don't want to share their land with Jews, or like, since the Arabs don't want the Jews, the Jews are simply taking the Arabs' land for themselves. I don't want to be a part of it either way. If there isn't a war here now, there will be, and in all wars one side takes from the other, or, how do you say it in Latin, *vice versa?*

179

"Hymie, that's absurd," I tell him. "The property the Jews have settled on has all been bought and paid for by the Jewish National fund and other organizations."

"'Maybe that is so now,' he retorts,' but when the coming war is over, we'll see how things look then. We'll see who's on whose land then! No matter how they look, I didn't come here to be a part of a war between Jews and Arabs. I came to bring refugees to Palestine because it was the only place they had to go.'"

"Hymie," I ask. "Are you sure that what you learned at Kfar Giladi about things being *complicated* only had to do with the Arab Israeli situation?" Bloom lets out a long sigh. "It's the only really big argument your father and I ever had. We disagreed vehemently. But I wish I hadn't said that last thing to him.

"There were plenty of other points to argue. Things like how can you call yourself a Jew Hymie, if you don't believe this land is the home of the Jews. We have a deed to it, and the deed is in the Bible! Zion is referred to over and over again in the Torah and in our prayers for the last two thousand years. I think you are hiding your head in the ground like an ostrich hides its head when it doesn't want to see what's in front of it. But Hymie has an argument back to everything except the Leila complication.

"'I didn't say I don't think it's the home of the Jews. I think a Jew should live here if he wants to make his home here,' says Hymie. 'Sure, Jews have a right to live here. We should have that right because Jews have always lived here. It's the one place in the world they have always lived.'

"But you don't want to fight to make it a Jewish homeland."

"'No I do not, because others have always lived here too, and since that's the case, something needs to be worked out that satisfies the majority of the Jews and the majority of the Arabs living here, something peaceful.'

"But you don't understand Hymie. The Arabs don't

want any Jews living here unless the Arabs are in complete control. Oh yes, they say Jews can live here and have their civil rights and liberties, but the Arabs must be in complete control. That is just like it was for the Jews in Hungary before my family had to quit Hungary when it didn't turn out to be like that with universal rights, because the Hungarians felt they had to be in complete control after World War One. I didn't know you were a wide-eyed idealist. I thought you were a realist.

"After I said that, it was Hymie's turn to look at me silently, because there was nothing he could say to counter what I had said. But he didn't stop."

"'You may be correct,' he said. 'There are only a small handful of places in the world where Jews can live comfortably and be protected with full rights and privileges even though they are in the minority and a non-Jewish majority is in control, but I happen to live in one of those places. It's called the United States of America, and that's where I'm going, whether you choose to come back with me now, later or never. Call me an idealist, call me whatever you want.'

"And that's where our argument ended. Stubborn Hymie was the winner. He was going home, and I knew that I was going home with him. The question was, how were we going to get back to America?

"To do so, the first hurdle we had to scale was getting through the British controlled border crossings in order to exit Palestine. Unfortunately, almost every one of these meant crossing into places more dangerous to us than Palestine itself, Arab areas like Trans-Jordan or Egypt, which were still heavily influenced or controlled by Britain, or the Port Authority at Haifa, which was directly under British control. The Haganah would arrange false identities for us and false identity documents, but once we crossed out of Palestine, we would be on our own.

"It was decided the safest way out would be across the

border with Lebanon near Metula at the former *Nahal Ayyun* Bridge, which the British had rebuilt after it was destroyed by a military wing of Haganah known as the *Palmach.*

"'*Nahl Ayyun* is not heavily guarded, and it leads into Lebanon, a country formerly controlled by France. Lebanon is still under heavy French influence,' the Haganah officer who was advising us said. 'We are making false travel documents for you that you can use to get yourselves from there to France via ship from Tyre in Southern Lebanon. That will be easier for you than trying to get up to the port in Beirut or going over land through Turkey and Europe.

'When you get to France, you will go to a United States Consular office and tell them you have lost your passports. The French, of course, will be more friendly and open to you than anyone else. They are not so stiff and formal as the British because they are not on the verge of losing their empire like the British. They have already lost most of their empire. Of course, you will have to pay your way through all of this yourselves, including your transportation home.'

"That was the plan for getting out of Palestine," Bloom explained.

"That was the plan?" I asked this question because I was amazed at the possibilities for failure it contained.

"Yes, that was the plan. In those days you couldn't get on an El Al plane and just fly out of Israel to New York like you can today."

"Well, what kind of story were you going to give the U.S Consulate about losing your passports?"

"That was going to be the real problem, we knew, accounting for the amount of time we had spent outside of the United States. There was also another problem. We didn't have any money, and getting it wired to us from the United States wasn't going to be that easy."

TWENTY-TWO

"I never turn down a drink. Among friends it's always appropriate. A man is only a man as they say, but brandy is still brandy. You'll find that in the Talmud too."
Sholem Aleichem

"After meeting with a Haganah officer, we begin taking the steps necessary to follow the exit plan they have laid out for us. That, in itself, isn't easy. First, I go to the bank and open an account in my new assumed name. Then, I send Yetta a telegram with the new account number, telling her to wire the money we will need to my new bank account in my assumed name in Haifa. The telegram is signed in my alias with the initials H. B. after the signature, and although it's addressed to Mrs. Yetta Bloom, it begins with the salutation *Yettala meyn lib*, my term of endearment for her, so she will understand the telegram is really from me, not a hoax, and that she really should send the money.

"It wasn't easy on Yetta when I left to serve with Aliyah Bet. Because of the need for secrecy, I couldn't tell her what I was doing or where I was going. I simply told her I'd be away for a while, and that I'd be spending my time trying to help bring a new Jewish state into existence. She accepted this because she, like me, believed in Zionism ardently. But my absence took its toll on her I'm sure, and I wasn't certain just how she'd respond to my telegram asking for money, especially since I omitted the fact that I was coming home, and that the money was needed so I could come home.

"Hymie, on the other hand, simply wrote Anne for money directly, but against my advice he was less

183

circumspect than me. He told her about Aliyah Bet; that he was now in Palestine; and that he needed money to pay for his way home. I'm sure this information shocked her, as she had no idea he was going to engage in running refugees into Palestine. She was under the impression that he had gone to Europe to look for family and relatives who had been war victims. I'm sure that when he revealed the complete truth to her it had an effect on their relationship. In any event, he never heard back from her.

"Eventually, Yetta wired the money for which I'd asked to my new bank account, but Hymie never received anything from Anne. It became evident that I was going to have to foot not only my own expenses, but also the bills he incurred in getting out of the Middle East.

'I swear I will pay you back,' he promised.

'Of course you will,' I said. 'So I will loan you the money. This is what friends are for.'

"After communicating with our wives, Hymie and I take the bus up to Metula together so we can cross into Lebanon from there. Part of the reason the Haganah thinks it will be easier to get out of Palestine and into Lebanon through Metula is the "Good Neighbor" agreement. This agreement was signed between France and Britain in 1926, after the French ceded the settlement at Metula to the British. The agreement permits Metula's farmers to cross the border with special "transit documents" into Lebanese territory so they can farm their fields which lay on the French-controlled Lebanese side of the border.

"Among the false documents the Haganah has prepared for us are two of these temporary transit documents portraying us as Metula farmers who supposedly will cross into Lebanon to tend our fields. Once across the border, we will instead just keep going. Arrangements have been made for Haganah operatives to meet us in Metula and show us the transit points at the border.

"We arrive in Metula on a very grey day. It reminds

Hymie of the time he has spent there before, and he doesn't
like it all. All seems very glum until, lo and behold, who do
we find is there to assist us? Eitan and Dani, the medic from
Kfar Giladi who tended to Leila when she died. Crying,
Hymie hugs them both. It's like a homecoming for him.
Eitan is also very emotional, gesturing in the air with his
hands as he chatters away in French, although neither of us
can understand. His face is very young, his curly hair is very
black and wild, but his eyes are still dull and filmy from
grief, almost like those of a Lake Erie Walleye. Dani
translates for us as we sit down to have tea with them.

 'I didn't know you were Haganah when I was at Kfar
Giladi, Hymie,' Eitan says. 'Yet we were fighting there, side
by side.'

 "'So Chaim, you are leaving us,' Dani asks."

 "Hymie nods 'yes,' and casts his eyes downward, as if
he's ashamed.'

 "'I can understand that,' says the medic. 'You and your
friend here have made your contributions to *Eretz Ysroel* by
trying to bring us refugees on your American ship, and
Chaim, you've even fought for our country during your time
at Kfar Giladi like the good kibbutznik you turned out to be.
So now you can go home in good conscience, eh? You have
done us a *mitzvah* and you should be proud.'

 'I wasn't trying to do anybody a good deed,' Hymie
replies. 'I only did it because I felt it was the right thing to
do.'

 'Yes,' says the medic. And this is exactly what a
mitzvah is isn't it—the right thing to do!'

 "Eitan then says something in French, and thrusts two
cartons of Lucky Strikes at us. 'He wants you to have these,'
Dani says. 'He thinks that even if you don't smoke, you'll be
able to use them to broker small favors from the Arabs along
the way. Remember, in this part of Lebanon many of the
Arabs are Christians, and they will want to help you if you
befriend them.'

'But most of them are Shiite Muslims,' Eitan tries to say in English. He can understand a little English, but when he tries to speak he has to switch to French.'

"Small maps are then pulled out and we are given simple hand-held compasses. The two Palestinian Jews then instruct us where to go and what routes we are to take once we are in Lebanon. When we cross the border, we will be only a few kilometers from the Litani River where it takes a sharp bend to the west as it flows from the north of Lebanon. We are to find this bend and follow the river to the west to where it flows into the Mediterranean. Then we are to turn south. Within ten kilometers of our turn to the south we will reach the city of Tyre. In Tyre, we are to locate the harbor-master; show him our money; and, say, *'Nous voulons un bateau a Marseille,'* meaning 'We want a boat to Marseilles.' If he can understand us, he will help us.

"With Eitan's guidance, we practice saying it over and over again until he thinks the harbor-master has a chance of understanding us. *'Nous voulouns un bateau a Marseille. Nous voulouns un bateau a Marseille.'* Finally, Eitan thinks we have the accent good enough. He tells Dani, however, to tell Hymie to let me do the talking in Tyre because Hymie's combination Yiddish/Russian accent is too heavy for a French speaker to understand.

"We all have a good laugh about that. The next morning, we rise early and ready ourselves to leave. But before he sets us on our way, Eitan drives Hymie and me down to Kfar Giladi in a jeep, and we visit Leila's grave in the darkness of the morning. Dani goes with us to translate. Nobody at the kibbutz is up yet.

'Eitan wants to know if you want to see his and Leila'a son before you go,' the medic asks.

'No. I should just go.' Hymie replies. The emotion of the situation is obviously getting to him.

"We then drive back to the border crossing; say good-by; and cross the border from Metula. We cross without incident on the strength of our temporary transit documents and our disguises as farmers. The sun is just coming up, and the other farmers from Metula are there to cross with us. It's going to be a beautiful day. Hymie is humming something.

'What is that,' I ask?

'It's a song I learned from Leila—*Artza Alenu*.' It's obvious he's not concentrating on getting across the border, even though that's what he previously insisted on doing in order to leave Palestine, and that's the very thing we're doing now. Instead, at this moment, Hymie's thoughts are with Leila.

"Once across the border, I ask a Jewish farmer who has crossed with us named Yonaton how far it is to the westward bend in the Litani. He tells me it's about four kilometers away and points in the direction of the river. He explains that there's a castle at the river's edge called Beaufort Castle, and that across the river is a Shiite Arab village called Kafar Tebnit.

Hymie and I wait for all the farmers to set about their work, and then we head off in the direction Yonaton has pointed. For the first kilometer we are among the fields of the Jewish farmers. But after we leave the cultivated fields, the terrain gets rough and rocky. The hills make it hard to walk. When we reach the river we are relieved, and we begin to follow it to the West. But the landscape gets worse. At times the river seems almost to be far below us in a deep gorge. This trip is not going to be easy.

"We decide the best way to traverse the eighteen kilometer distance to the city of Tyre from the bend in the river would actually be by boat on the river itself. There are rowboats tied up at many of the small villages we pass along the river, but we don't want to steal one. That would only run the risk of attracting unwanted attention. Without being able to speak Arabic, however, we can't make anybody understand that we would like to buy a boat. Finally, when we reach the tiny Shiite village of Kfar Sir, one of the locals realizes we are willing to pay in prized American dollars and he agrees to sell us his boat. He is also interested in our cartons of Lucky Strikes, which he can sell at a premium, so we toss those in as part of the price for the boat. Handing him the two cartons of Lucky Strikes we have with us makes the entire transaction go much more smoothly, even though there is a huge language barrier.

"The boat makes the rest of our trip much easier. Even so, it turns out that our trip from Metula to Tyre is going to take two days, which means a camp-out overnight. We will have to sleep somewhere along the way, and we decide to do so under the stars in the boat. During the night we can look up and see the millions of stars in the Milky Way, and we can hear the shepherds quietly tending their sheep on the hills.

"The Haganah's assessment concerning our best escape route from Palestine turns out to be correct. With Lebanon being a former French protectorate, as opposed to a British protectorate, and having been an independent nation since November 1943, we encounter no difficulties, militarily, bureaucratically or otherwise, moving through the country. The fact that this new little country is a political amalgam of Maronite Christians, Shiite Arabs and Sunni Muslims doesn't hurt either. Ever since France's power was completely and finally wrested from Lebanon in mid-1946 with the withdrawal of the last French troops, the local government, with varying degrees of success, has liberally attempted to tolerate persons of varying nationalities and religions, unlike most other Arab countries in the Middle East, although Lebanon did wind up joining the Arab League.

"The next day, we reach the ancient Phoenician city of Tyre. There, our fraudulent travel documents from Lebanon to France are accepted by the harbor-master, who is trying to be very gracious to us, without asking too many questions. He puts us in touch with the French ship-line *Compagnie*

Generale Transatlantique (C GT), and when language
becomes a barrier between us and the French, he arranges for
an interpreter for us. We stay the night in Tyre, waiting for
our ship to arrive.

"In the morning we are on our way to Marseille.
Hymie's relief is tangible—no more displaced person's
camps on Cyprus; no more Athlit; no more dealing with the
polite British and the implicit threats of legal action and
incarceration they hold over him; and, no more Arab attacks
like the one at Kfar Giladi.

"On board the ship we plan our next moves. We know
it will be necessary to explain our long absences from the
United States when we appear at the U.S. Consulate Office
in France claiming our passports are lost. The question is,
what stories are we going to make up to tell them? We
decide that for men of our age it will be necessary to disguise
ourselves, but what disguises will be believable? In any
event, new clothes will be necessary. In Marseilles, we plan
to go shopping for new clothes.

"We could dress as businessmen in suits, but it would be
too easy for the embassy to check out the business contacts
we tell them we had when we are interrogated. We could
invent stories of travel and romantic adventures in Europe,
but we know we are a little too old to make such stories
appear believable. Thinking of Leila, we realize how ironic
this is. But it's almost a certainty that no young consulate
officer is going to believe we were engaged in romantic
liaisons. There is a possibility we could say we were
working for the Jewish Agency in Europe to bringing relief
to the displaced persons there, but the Agency might prefer
to wash its hands of such a tale and have nothing to do with
us because of the dangers inherent in being involved in
illegal immigration at the time.

"Finally, we hit on a story that we think will stick
because it can't be checked out. We will tell them we spent
late 1946 and most of 1947 drinking hard, and moving

between casinos in Monaco and Casablanca to gamble, and that our passports were either stolen or lost on our last trip back to France from Morocco.

"So in Marseilles, we shop for dandy's clothes to make ourselves look like gamblers—striped but muted double-breasted suits with big padding in the shoulders, high wasted pants with pleats and cuffs cut broad around the ankle, broad silk neckties with large geometric or art deco patterns in bright colors, shirts with pointed collars, two toned black and white shoes, sock garters, trench coats and fedoras. For myself, I choose a homburg instead of a fedora.

"At the Consulate Office, the consular officer, listens to our stories and to Hymie's accent; asks us if we won or lost at the casinos; takes one look at Hymie's hands which are still grimy under his nails and cut up from working in the engine room of the Tradewinds; and remarks that our clothes look amazingly new even though we tell him we lost in the casinos. Then he laughs and says:

'If you guys are really going to try to make us believe you spent all this time in Monaco and Casablanca gambling as you say, you would have done better to come in here wearing tuxedos. That would have been a better costume for you.'

'Are we in trouble,' Hymie whispers to me?

'I don't know yet,' I say.

'So tell me,' the consular officer says. 'You guys say you're from Cleveland, Ohio? I also am from Cleveland. So I have a little test for you. So tell me—who plays third base for the Cleveland Indians?'

'Al Rosen,' I say.

'And short stop?'

'Lou Boudreau,' Hymie chimes in.

'Name Three of their best pitchers.' the consular officer demands.

'Bob Lemon, Mike Garcia and Bob Feller,' we say in unison.

'And their center fielder?'

'Larry Doby,' I say

'What is the tallest building in Cleveland called?'

'The Terminal Tower,' Hymie responds.

"The consulate officer then looks up and mumbles, "OK, you pass.' He then stamps all our papers, and provides us with travel documents, valid for a one-way trip to the United States only. He looks at us and says, 'Gentlemen, in all my time sitting behind this desk, I find your stories to be among the most creative I've ever heard—two hard drinking gamblers—Hmph.'

"He then picks up the phone. Listening to his phone conversation, I realize he is assigning an official to escort us from Marseilles to Paris by train, and there to place us directly on board an aircraft to New York.

"'I am going to arrange for you to be detained by the United States Customs Service in New York,' he says. 'They will bring in any other agencies they deem necessary to interrogate you when you arrive. Until your train leaves for Marseilles you will remain as our guests here in this office. I trust you will find that satisfactory. We own the building and our marines guard it.'

'Yes,' we tell him. 'That will be most satisfactory to us.'

TWENTY-THREE

"The menace of communism in this country will remain a menace until the American people make themselves aware of the techniques of communism. No one who truly understands what it really is can be taken in by it. Yet the individual is handicapped by coming face to face with a conspiracy so monstrous he cannot believe it exists. The American mind simply has not come to a realization of the evil which has been introduced into our midst. It rejects even the assumption that human creatures could espouse a philosophy which must ultimately destroy all that is good and decent."

J. Edger Hoover

"The customs agents at the New York airport immediately turn us over to the F.B.I. when we land. We are taken from LaGuardia into Manhattan by two agents who have very official looking badges and guns in shoulder holsters, and we are ensconced in a room without windows on the eighteenth floor of the F.B.I.'s New York Divisional Headquarters. The room has a mirror mounted along one wall, which I presume is a two-way mirror, and there is a stark grey metal table in the center, with two wooden slatted-back chairs on either side of it. Hymie and I sit together on the same side. There is a telephone on the table.

"An agent enters the room, offering us cigarettes, which we refuse, and water, which we accept. He introduces himself as Agent William Oakley and tells us he's going to ask us a few questions, which shouldn't take too long, and then we can probably be on our way. 'So,' he says, turning to Hymie. 'What is your name, and I mean your real name?'

"'Hyman,-- actually – Chaim-- Zeltzer,' your father answers."

"'And where were you born,' the agent asks?'

"'Kherson'

"'Kherson. Isn't that in the U.S.S.R?'

"'The Ukraine'

"'Well, I meant the Soviet Union of Socialist Republics—they're all the same now, aren't they?'

"'No,' I don't think so,' says Hymie.

"The agent enters some notes on the legal pad he has with him, and then says, 'But you are a citizen of the United States, are you not?'

"'Yes.'

"'And where were you naturalized'

"'Rochester, New York.' More notes are scribbled on the pad, and he then picks up the phone and tells someone on the other end of the line to contact the branch F.B.I. office in Albany for a naturalization check. 'The name is Hyman, or Chaim, Zelitzer and the point of entry was Rochester.' He now spells it Zeltzer, Z-E-L-T-Z-E-R.

"'And you sir,--your name?' The agent says looking at me."

"Herschel Bloom.

"'But is that your real name sir? I need your real name.

"Blumenshtein."

"'What?"

"My real name is Herschel Tsvi Blumenshtein, and I was born in a city called Brasov, which is in Romania now."

"'That is communist Romania, is it not?"

"Not back then."

"'But now it is, is it not?"

I interrupt Bloom at this point and tell him that it sounds to me like this agent has got a thing on his mind about communists, not about Aliyah Bet and the illegal immigration of DPs. Otherwise why is he taking such an

193

interest in where Herschel and my father were born when they've both been naturalized citizens of the United States for over thirty years? Bloom reminds me that back then in the late forties and all the way through the fifties, everybody in this country was worried about the communists and the Cold War that had broken out with the Soviet Union.

He explains it was the time when McCarthyism was waxing strongly all over the country, and alleged American traitor communists like Alger Hiss were being hung out to dry by the F.B.I. and by supposedly repatriated former communists the likes of Whittacker Chambers. It was a time when F.B.I Director, J. Edgar Hoover was looking for communists under every bush in order to build his reputation, and when the F.B.I. was hot on the trails of the notorious traitors Julius and Ethel Rosenberg.

"Of course, it also didn't help any," Bloom adds, "that many Jews in this country were automatically suspect of being communists at the time, or that the New York Field Office of the F.B.I. was a major focus for FBI counterintelligence efforts during World War Two, liaising with British intelligence through the British Security Coordination Office."

He goes on to explain that after the war, the British were outraged by the bad publicity they were receiving because of the Exodus Affair and the increased pressure Aliyah Bet was putting on them to open Jewish immigration to Palestine. So they launched a major propaganda campaign alleging communist influence in the Middle East was growing because the Soviet Union had opened the floodgates of Jewish immigration from Romania. "As you will see from the treatment your father and I received as the story goes on, the New York F.B.I. Branch Office was significantly affected by that British campaign."

"Go on with the story then," I tell him.

"Well after this agent has pumped us for every conceivable detail of our foreign backgrounds—like why did

my family leave Brasov for Hungary; why did we leave
Hungary; how did your father end up coming to the United
States from Kherson; is the rest of his family still in the
U.S.S.R; etc. etc.—he moves to another subject. He takes
down all the information he can get about where we live in
the States, what our wives' names are, who are friends are,
what we did to earn our livings before we went to Europe,
and what are social security numbers are. He also wants to
know our military histories.

"Then he says, 'I'm informed that the two of you are
supposed to be professional gamblers or something like that,
and that you were moving about from place to place in
Europe and North Africa playing Roulette and Bacara, I
don't know the game called Bacara. Can one of you explain
it to me please?'

"Neither of us knew how to play Bacara, so I answered.
'That was not our game. We played European Blackjack.'"

"'Oh,' he said, 'and what are the differences between
European and American Blackjack?'"

"I was able to explain the differences between European
and American Blackjack to him because of a book I'd once
read on the subject."

"'Nicely done,' he says. 'But I don't really believe you
spent all that time you were overseas gambling. Have you
got anything to prove it? Some chip receipts perhaps, or
money exchange documents from a casino, or even a coat
check or a hotel bill?'"

"We had nothing. Our silence was deafening."

"'Ok boys,' the agent says. 'We're gonna sit here until
you tell us what you were doing over there in Europe for all
that time, and if we can't get it out of you, we're gonna
interview your wives and all your friends until we find out.'"

"When Hymie hears this he cracks. He doesn't want the
F.B.I coming around to interview his wife in Cleveland. He
figures it will scare her, but mostly he figures he's already in
enough trouble with her. 'We were in the Aliya Bet,' he

says."

"I give him a look that could kill because he's revealing this secret organization."

"'The Aliyah what,' says Agent Oakley?"

"'Aliyah Bet. There's nothing illegal about it in this country, or about what we did while we were in it. We didn't break any of the laws of the United States.' Hymie's up on his muscle now, giving it back to our interrogator in spades. 'You've got to let us go. We did nothing wrong,' he says."

"'We'll see about that gentlemen,' Agent Oakley replies. 'Just wait here. I'll be back in a few minutes.' Then he leaves the room.

"He returns with a swarthy little Mediterranean looking man and introduces him to us as Judah Reichman,the New York Division's expert on elicit dealings with Palestinian Jews."

"'So tell me,' Reichman says, 'What can you tell us about Hotel Fourteen on 60th Street in Manhattan?' Hymie and I exchange blank stares."

"'Well let me give you a hint. What famous night club occupied the basement of that building?' Again we stare at each other blankly. 'So do you know a man named Reuven Zaslansky, alias Reuven Shiloah?'"

"We both say 'no.'"

"No, well what about Jacob Dostrovsky, alias Yaakov Dori. Do you know who he is?"

"Again we are silent."

"Hmph! You expect us to believe you were in the Aliyah Bet and yet you don't know any of these people or any of these places? Well, tell me—have you ever heard of David Ben-Gurion?"

"Yes," we both shout."

"'Oh, him you've heard of—well hallelujah! But you don't know that Reuven Shiloah was in America organizing support for the Haganah, in 1946, or that Yaakov Dori acquired the ships for the American Aliyah Bet. How do you expect us to believe that you had anything to do with the Aliyah Bet?' Reichman then scrapes his chair back and gets up to leave."

'But we *were* in Aliyah Bet,' Hymie insists. Our ship was the <u>Tradewinds,</u> later known as the *Hatikvah.* We were recruited by Danny Schind and . . . '

"'Schind? You knew Schind,' Reichman interrupts?'"

"'. . . yes, he is also known as Ze'ev Danny Schind,' Hymie says."

"And who was Schind working with?"

"A man named Captain . . .

"I grab Hymie's arm and hold my forefinger up to my lips telling him to be quiet. I didn't want him giving out Captain Ash's name because he was an American, who could easily be taken into custody by the authorities. He was not a Palestinian Jew. The F.B.I. seemed to know about Aliyah Bet, but I didn't know how much they knew, and it was not our place to leak any more information to them than they already had."

Bloom then interrupts himself to explain that later, after the interrogation, my father and he learned that the club in the basement of Hotel Fourteen to which Richman was referring, was the Copacabana. It was where all the Haganah operatives who came to New York met to hatch their plans for raising American support for their paramilitary organization. Reuven Zalansky, later the Chief of Shin Bet, Israel's General Security Service, came there in early 1946 to organize American support for the Haganah.

Arrangements were made for him to stay at Hotel Fourteen by Fanny Barnett, who had worked at the Jewish Agency in New York, and her husband Rudy Barnett, two American Zionists who had earlier purchased Hotel Fourteen. When the Jewish Palestinians stayed in New York, they stayed in room 300 of the Hotel Fourteen while conferring with their American friends. Room 300, later

David Selcer

known as "Kibbutz 14" became the clandestine meeting place of many of the future leaders of Israel, all of whom the F. B. I. was trying to watch. It was in Room 300 that Yaacov Dori worked on his secret mission to acquire and see to the refitting of ships for the Aliyah Bet. Dori later became Israel's first military chief of staff. Danny Schind came to New York to help him ready the Secret Fleet of the Jews for action. He also spent many hours in Room 300 at Hotel Fourteen.

TWENTY-FOUR

"When the heart is full it runs out of the eyes."
Sholem Aleichem

Then the interrogation started to get very intense.
Bloom goes on to say that Reichman kept hammering at him,
though his questions were not very penetrating. "What do
you know about the Sonneborn Institute," he demanded to
know?

'Nothing,' Bloom answered. 'What is it?'

'Did you ever attend any meetings of the Sonneborn
Institute?'

'I don't even know what it is,' Bloom insisted.

'Have you ever met Rudolf G. Sonneborn?'

'No.'

'Do you know where the Hotel McAlpin is?'

'No. Is it in New York? I'm not from New York.'

'Then I don't suppose you met there for lunch on
Thursdays with members of the Sonneborn Institute for
discussions about what needed to be done next for Aliyah
Bet.'

'That is correct.'

'It seems you don't know anything at all about Aliyah
Bet. Are you sure the two of you were members of that
organization?'

'Very sure.'

"At this point, says Bloom, Reichman breaks off the
interrogation and leaves the room. 'Hymie is scared to
death. 'What's he talking about,' your poor father asks? Do
you know about any of this?'"

199

"Don't worry, Hymie,' I tell him. 'He's just trying to impress us with the fact that they know more about Aliyah Bet than we think they do. He's trying to scare us. But what he doesn't understand is that we truly don't know anything about the stuff he's talking about. I think he's talking about some really big contributors high up in the United Jewish Appeal or something like that, but I really don't know for sure.'"

Then Reichman re-enters the room, according to Bloom, and says, 'Alright, maybe we are going about this in the wrong way. Maybe you guys are too far down the Aliyah Bet food chain to know any of the people I'm talking about or any of the places I've mentioned, but what kind of evidence can you give me that you were actually with the Aliyah Bet? I'm looking for documentary evidence and the names of other Aliyah Bet members, particularly Americans that you know.'

Bloom's first inclination, he says, is to tell the F.B.I. about the acceptance letters Aliyah Bet sent my father and him, inviting them to Baltimore to join the crew of the Tradewinds, but these letters are signed by an American citizen, Dewey Stone, the sole stockholder of Captain Ash's Weston Trading Company. Bloom knows Stone to be a prominent businessman, philanthropist and community leader from Brockton, Massachusetts, and is very concerned about implicating any American citizens, other than my father or himself in Aliyah Bet's activities. Stone, among other things is the conduit for American financial contributions spent by Aliyah Bet, and the acceptance letters are written on Weston Trading Company stationery. That will also implicate Captain William C. Ash, as well as Dewey Stone.

Finally, he agrees that he will turn over the half-sheet agreement both men signed showing that they were agreeing to serve on "the ship known as Tradewinds sailing under the flag of Panama from Baltimore without pay. There are no

names on these papers other than Pa's and Bloom's, and
there is no address other than a Post Office Box in
Washington D.C.

"Then, surprisingly," as Bloom relates it, "the F.B.I
agreed to let us go, but with the understanding that we and
our families would still continue to be investigated. It was a
long day," he says, and he tries to explain why he thinks the
federal police gave us so much attention.

Not only was the F.B.I. mandated, under the reign of J.
Edgar Hoover, to investigate all possible contacts between
American citizens and Russian communists, but, as Bloom
explains it, that's particularly what the federal agency
wanted to look into concerning my father and him. It wasn't
because Hyman Zeltzer was a Russian, and it wasn't because
he and Bloom were Jews. It was because the U.S.
Department of State and the F.B.I. were particularly
interested in determining on which side of the Iron Curtain
the emerging Middle Eastern countries were likely to align
themselves, particularly the new state the Jews were trying to
build in Palestine.

"If we were truly in Aliyah Bet," says Bloom, "The
F.B.I. was going to thoroughly check out the question of
whether we had been in contact with any communists. 1944
had seen the adoption of a pro-Zionist policy by Russia's
Joseph Stalin, who believed that if and when Israel came into
existence, it would be socialist, and it would facilitate the
downfall of Britain's influence in the Middle East. The
Brits, themselves, believed that the European refugees were
in league with the communists for the same reasons. They
even spread rumors to that effect. Indeed, in November
1947, the Soviet Union, together with the other Sovirt bloc
countries voted in favor of the United Nations Partition Plan
for Palestine, which paved the way for the creation of Israel
and the exit of the British from that area. The idea that
Bolshevism and the Jews were conflated had also been
heavily propagated by the Nazis during World War Two, and

by the White Russians before them, during Russia's Civil War between the Reds (Bolsheviks) and the Whites (Mensheviks)."

. . .

Where Palestine might fall on the chess board between the East and the West was the last thing on my father's and Herschel's minds, however, as they emerged back into the daylight on the streets of New York from the windowless office in the F.B.I. Divisional Headquarters where they had been detained for an entire day. They were more worried about their next strategic encounters—meeting up with their wives after being away secretly for a year and a half.

"It wasn't going to be easy," Bloom said. "Think of it for a minute—you're a woman who's been married to the same man for thirty-five years, and suddenly your husband tells you he has to go away for a while, but he can't tell you for how long, or where he's going, and he tells you what he's going to be doing while he's away only in the vaguest terms. He says things like, 'I'm going to be helping to resettle war refugees,' or. 'I'm going to Europe to look for my lost family,' or, 'I've been asked to assist in setting up a new business entity, but it must be kept secret for a while or others will steal the idea. I can't tell you a thing about what I'll be doing.'"

"Wouldn't you feel that you were being abandoned? That's what Hymie and I were up against. And even when we came back, there still weren't many details we could really get into about our absence.

The F.B.I. continued asking questions back in Cleveland, and their agents seemed to be showing up everywhere and checking out everything: the Blooms' farm; the Blooms' friends; the Zeltzers' grocery; their customers. It was particularly disturbing that they shadowed customers of the grocery and interviewed them. They just kept on intruding, relentlessly asking questions. They hadn't ended their investigation. They had simply transferred it to Cleveland.

Herschel and Hymie didn't care, but they soon found out their wives did. According to Bloom, the story went this way.

"Yetta and Anne were waiting for us on the platform at the Union Terminal underneath Cleveland's Terminal Tower, as we emerged from our Pullman car after taking the train overnight. We had come in on the Ohio State Limited. Anne had called Yetta, excitedly telling her she had received a call from Hymie who said we were together in New York and would be arriving at noon the next day. So Yetta drove in from Mentor, picked up Anne, and the two of them were waiting for us when we arrived. After exchanging excited greetings, the four of us went out for coffee together at the Cleveland Arcade. Almost immediately, the subject of the F.B.I. came up.

"'Hymie,' Anne said. 'Policemen have been coming to the store and asking me questions about you. I don't like it.'

'What have they been wanting to know?'

'They knew you were in Palestine! You were observed there taking a bus to some place called Metula with a woman who may have been Haganah, and they wanted to know who she was. I didn't tell them anything because I didn't know anything, not even what is Haganah.'

"Hymie immediately turned sheepish," said Bloom. "He blushed, if you could say a man can do that, and then he said, 'Yes, I didn't get a chance . . .

'You never told me you were going to Palestine, Hymie. I only found out from your last letter to me which came from there, saying you were working for an organization called Aliyah Bet and you were coming home soon.'

' . . . to tell you I was there.' His voice trailed off. Then he cleared his throat and collected himself. 'Yes, well you see, from Cyprus they took us to a detention camp in Palestine, and . . .

'A detention camp! You never told me you were in a detention camp! I thought you were traveling with Bori's cousin who you found in Italy, and you went to Cyprus together where everything was good and comfortable, as you said in the letter I got from you.'

'. . . and in Palestine I found a big surprise for you I've been waiting to tell you about. Anne, I found out your father had been to Palestine. He may still be there.'

"Hymie was trying to change the subject—to deflect Anne's attention away from the issue of the woman he was with on the bus to Metula—but it wasn't going very well for him. With every word he said, he just dug himself deeper and deeper into a hole."

"'My father,' said Anne. 'You found my father? Well, surely you would have written me from Palestine to tell me that. But you didn't. Was he in this place called Metula?'

'No, I didn't say that, Anne. I didn't say I actually *found* your father. I said I found *evidence* that your father had been to Palestine. You see, while I was in the detention camp, I saw his name carved on the wall of one of the barracks-- *Rebbe Israel Fogel – Stanislawow – Galitzia – 1938.'*

'And you didn't go look for him, even though you were in Palestine where you saw this? You didn't write me about it? Why not? Instead you go to Metula with this Haganah woman, and then you tell me you're coming home!'

"Anne was getting indignant," says Bloom, "and I thought I'd better jump in to try to help your father out. There were tears forming in her grey eyes. Things weren't going well for Hymie at all. The hole he was digging for himself was just getting deeper."

"It was a prison camp, Anne," I said. "Athlit was a prison camp. He just couldn't go out and look for your father."

'But if he was seen on a bus going somewhere, he was out of the prison camp already. I don't understand any of this,' Anne snapped. 'What was the name of this camp?'

'Athlit,' Hymie replied.

'I still don't understand,' she said. 'Why were you even there? Why would my father have been there? Why were you in Palestine, and you didn't even write to let me know you were in that country until you were ready to come home?'

"It was becoming obvious that Hymie had left home, telling Anne practically nothing about what he was going to be doing or where he would be going. He had left her almost totally in the dark. Even my Yetta was now getting upset with him. She knew, in a very general sense, a lot more than Anne knew about what we had been doing while we were gone, because before I left I told her about Aliyah Bet and why it existed, and I told her I was joining, but that she must never discuss this with anyone because that would bring danger to me.

"Apparently, she took this so literally that she never even told Anne about it, even though when she heard Hymie had left home, she suspected he was with me. Don't forget, Yetta and I were Zionists. We had long supported the Zionist cause together. Even before I left, she knew I had attended various Zionist functions and meetings and that I had given financial support to many Zionist organizations.

"Anne and Hymie, however, were not Zionists. So Anne had no reason to know the importance of secrecy concerning what we were attempting to do. Yetta knew that Anne was very gregarious, and Yetta very much feared that if she told Anne anything at all about what I was doing or where I might be, it would get out and perhaps become public knowledge. So she said nothing about it to Anne.

"But when she saw how disturbed Anne was becoming listening to all of this about her father, about Hymie's not telling her he was in Palestine until he was ready to leave, and about the Athlit prison camp, she suddenly turned to Anne and said, 'Anne, perhaps I have not been as good a friend as I should have been to you. I suspected Hymie was with Herschel in Europe and in the Middle East all along, but I never said anything to you, even when you were telling me how much you missed him. It was because I knew how important secrecy was to the Aliyah Bet. For this, I apologize. I did not know any specifics of what they were doing anyways. I only knew generally what was going on.'"

"Yetta's confession to Anne turned what originally had been intended as just a welcome home cup of coffee between friends into a three-hour dinner during which Hymie and I revealed to both of them much of what we had been doing while we were away. Yetta asked many questions, but Anne mostly just sat there quietly listening. Then she began crying."

Bloom tells me that this last story about their homecoming concludes *Da Ault Geshikhtem.* "So what, if anything, have you learned from these stories," he asks?

"What have I learned?" I pause a long time to think. "Mostly, that sons grow up when they stop blaming their fathers' mistakes for their lot in life and start making different mistakes on their own."

"I don't understand," he says

"You will," I reply, "if you think about the things I've said about Pa during my stay here, as well as what you've told me about my father."

I decide it's time for me to go home. I thank him profusely for all the time he has taken with me, and I tell him that what he has said has given me a new vision of my father, one that commands much more respect than my own vision of him had previously commanded. Pa was not just an uneducated peasant as I had always thought. His seeming obliviousness to many things no longer concealed from me the fact that he actually had ideals by which he lived, a philosophy, and that these principles controlled his life. He was brave, honest, strong and persevering. He cared about others and he had heart. There was nothing evil about him. Nor was there anything simple. He didn't want to be one of those persons who just puts in his time on earth making himself as comfortable as possible, and then dies. Indeed, he raised a family, worked very hard, participated in great adventures, and he managed to help found a nation, whether he knew it or not. The only thing that bothered me now were the questions I had about Leila, the woman he had met in Palestine. What kind of relationship did they actually have?

I got in the car and rushed home to tell my wife all about the things I learned while at Bloom's farm. Excitedly, I tell Sonia about all of it, except what happened between Pa and Leila in her room before the morning of the battle at Kibbutz Kfar Giladi. I just can't bring myself to reveal that part of the *Alt Geshikthem* to her.

TWENTY-FIVE

*"There is nothing in the world, I tell you, so maddening
as a person who doesn't answer when you abuse him. You
shout and you scold, you are ready to burst a gut, and he
stands there and smiles..."*

-- Sholem Aleichem

I knew there was more for me to learn about what
happened between my mother and father after the last story,
and about why Ma was so reluctant to talk about it. Bloom
just couldn't tell me about any of that because he wasn't
present to witness it when it happened, and he therefore
knew nothing of it. The rest, I would have to get directly
from my mother if I could get her to talk about it

During the drive back to Akron, I decided I should wait
a long time before bringing the issue of The Old Stories up
to my mother. I figured that by now she knew all or most of
them well, having heard them, if not that night over dinner in
the Cleveland Arcade, at least over the years before Pa died.
I also knew the things in these stories were like an open
wound to her. She felt Pa had just abandoned her for a year
and a half.

What I couldn't surmise was whether she had ever
discussed the issue of Leila with him, and I didn't know how
I could even broach that subject with her. Surely, I knew
now that Pa was no fool. What man would ever discuss such
a thing with his wife, except a fool? And yet, if I had learned
anything from The Old Stories, I had learned that my father
was a very moral man with a conscience. Hard as it might
be to believe, maybe he had voluntarily admitted how he

spent his time with Leila and begged for Ma's forgiveness.

All I knew for sure was that it was too soon after the funeral to talk about any of the specifics of The Old Stories with Ma. *Da Alt Geshikhtem* obviously had a profound effect on her, and they were not something which could be discussed with her without delicacy. I decided that instead, I would just have to speak with her about things she and Pa did after he came home, and wait to see if she ever brought up The Old Stories herself.

About two months later, without any motive other than curiosity, I hit upon a subject that occurred after Pa came back from Palestine. "Ma," I asked one day when I was in Cleveland visiting, "Why did you and Pa decide to move to Florida?"

"Miami," she said? "It was a present your father gave me."

"What do you mean by that, Ma?"

"Like a wedding present."

"A wedding present! Why would he give you a wedding present? By the time you moved to Miami, you had already been married for what: thirty-five or thirty-six years?"

"We were starting over, starting a brand new life, in a brand new place, with no more grocery business. I wasn't going to have to work anymore. I could just retire and, how do you call it-- socialize. We would sell the store and sell our double in Cleveland, and use the money to have a good time and to buy a house in Miami. Your father would start an egg business to bring in spending money. He got himself an egg delivery route and an old truck, and that was it. My gift was retirement, and I guess you could say, his gift was me. We just went off to the beautiful weather in Florida.

"By that time his two sisters, had also moved to Miami with their husbands from Detroit, so I had plenty of people to spend time with in Florida. It was really a happy time for me, and it was good for your Pa too. Miami reminded him of Odessa, which was a beautiful vacation spot near the city where he used to live when he was a child in Russia."

"But why do you refer to this all as a gift, Ma—a 'wedding present' as you call it, when you had already been married so long? Many couples retire, but when they do so, they just decide together that they're going to do it, and they do it together. Yet, you call it a gift to you from Pa. Why?"

"Because your father wasn't ready to retire. He would have just stayed in Cleveland where I'm sure he was very content to be."

"So did you ask him to move to Florida?"

"No."

"Then why did he decide to? Why do you call this 'a wedding present?'"

"Well that's a long story, one that I'd prefer not to get into."

I decided to tease her a little about this "wedding gift" thing, so I pushed on with it, thinking about how the rabbi had said at Pa's funeral what a good husband he was. In my mind I guess I was imagining that maybe my parents had experienced a re-emergence of their love for one another, or something like that, so they had decided to run off to Miami together. Whatever it was, how bad could it be to kid my mother a little about it?

"I wish you would, Ma," I said.

"Would what?"

"Tell me the story of Pa's wedding present to you. You make it sound like he was a real romantic or something, maybe like one of Sholem Aliechem's characters. Wasn't it Aleichem who wrote, '*Without love our life is . . . a ship without a rudder . . . like a body without a soul.*' Didn't the rabbi say at Pa's funeral that Pa read a lot of Sholem Aleichem?"

Ma suddenly became silent as I was kidding her. She just walked away—into the living room where she began playing with my boys and talking to Sonia. It was her way of changing the subject—just dropping it, without further ado. It was almost as if I'd hurt her feelings or something by trying to tease her. We ate dinner at her house that night, but not another word was said on the subject. In fact, not another word was said to me by Ma until we were leaving. Then she pulled me aside out of the hearing of the others.

"Lester." She said as her eyes teared up. "Lester let me tell you something. You have made me very angry. It is not for children to pry into the relationship of their parents. It's none of your business." She began walking away.

"Ma, I don't know what you mean. I wasn't prying. I was just . . .

"Now go!" She said, her speech very rapid, as she looked back. " And we will forget about this."

. . . trying to kid you."

. . .

In the car, on the way home, it hit me. Somehow my teasing may have touched on the final part of the story about why Ma would not discuss Pa's absence after World War Two—the grand finale, so to speak, to *Da Alt Geshikhtem.* What happened that was so painful to her she couldn't even discuss it while we were sitting *shiva* at Pa's funeral? Suddenly, I remembered one of Sholem Aleichem's other famous quotes. *"When the heart is full it runs out of the eyes."*

Leila! -- Did making a "present" of moving to Miami have something to do with Leila?

"You're awfully quiet," Sonia said as we drove back to Akron.

"I'm thinking."

"About what?"

"Do you remember when Ma and I were talking in the kitchen and she came into play with the boys in the living

211

room tonight, and you were there?"

"Not really."

"Well I know you and she gab with each other an awful lot when you're together. Did she say anything at all about me to you anytime tonight when I wasn't around?"

"Not really—just that 'Lester is acting like a silly little boy again.'"

"She said that?"

"Yes, she says it a lot—usually when you're complaining about your brother or saying something negative about your father. Were you doing that?"

"Tell me the circumstances. How did she happen to come to referring to me as a silly little boy tonight?"

"It was nothing really. She was just playing with the boys, and then for no reason she lost interest and started gazing out the window silently. I said, 'What's wrong Ma? Are you alright?' And she said, 'Nothing's wrong,' and then she made the remark about you being silly. That's all. Why, what's up?"

"I don't know if anything's up yet. I'll let you know if I find out. I think it has to do with their moving to Miami."

"They moved to Miami to retire Les. A lot of people do that. The real question is why'd they move back to Cleveland after all their time down there?"

"Oh that's an easy question Sonia. You know the answer. They moved back up north because Ben got sick again. You remember. But why did she get so bothered over being teased about Pa's present? That's not like her."

TWENTY-SIX

"In the name of Hypocrites, doctors have invented the most exquisite form of torture ever known to man: survival."
Edward Everett Hale

As Ben later told me, it was pouring when the ambulance, its siren screaming with flashing lights glaring, pulled into the emergency entrance at The Cleveland Clinic. Ma was transferred to a gurney; and the emergency physicians immediately fell to their work, even before she was in the door of the building. My brother parked his car and commenced pacing in the waiting room, just beyond the double doors to the inner emergency room. Evidently, he had been visiting Ma, and they had been arguing about something, when she suddenly crumpled to the floor unable to catch her breath.

We drove up to the hospital from Akron as soon as Ben called us to let us know she was there. It was raining the whole way up to Cleveland as we drove.

Ma was given aspirin but there was no relief. The cardiologist arrived. The decision was made to administer streptokinase, but the streptokinase did not stop her myocardia-infarction. Ma's heart attack continued without let up. So an emergency angiogram was ordered.

Finally, Sonia and I were allowed, with Ben, to go back to her bedside in the small curtained off emergency treatment room, but only for a moment, before she was to be taken to the cardiac catheterization laboratory. She was lying there, grey in the temples and colorless, with electrocardiogram leads clipped to her; an automatic blood pressure cuff in place; and a pulse fingertip oximeter attached. Oxygen was

213

being administered from a breathing tube in her nose, and a newly inserted I.V. was at the ready and waiting for the order of a physician to administer whatever might be needed.

The angiogram indicated significant arterial blockage so high up in her left anterior descending artery that it could not be stented. Instead, immediate coronary bi-pass surgery was necessary, and it was performed right then and there as she remained in the catheterization lab. After two and a half hours, that seemed like five, she was taken from surgery to recovery. The thoracic surgeon emerged from the lab to tell us that everything had gone about as well as it could go considering Ma's age and general health condition. They had cracked open her sternum to get to her heart, placed her on a heart-lung machine, and harvested a vein from her leg to be used as a by-pass from her aorta to below the blockage in the anterior descending artery of her heart.

"She should be alright, but we'll just have to wait and see," the surgeon said.

It was then that the real waiting started. Ben was beside himself. Agitated and nervous, he could not sit still in the lounge outside the recovery room. He refused to tell us what he and Ma had been arguing about. As for myself, the pure emotional trauma of the event had exhausted me. Pa had died six months ago. Now, was I also to lose my mother?

There was nothing to do but wait—wait and talk. And that's what Sonia and I did. She kept trying to take my mind off my fears.

"Remember the night we drove home from Cleveland Les,"she said, "wondering why your mother had blown up at you for teasing her about your father's supposedly making their move to Florida a wedding present to her?"

"Yes, I was just thinking about that," I said. "How coincidental that you would bring that up. What made you think of it just now?"

"I don't know, maybe you're telepathic. Maybe it was just coincidence, or maybe it's what believers in the

paranormal call synchronicity, or meaningful coincidence."
She smiled slyly. Sonia was a believer in the supernatural.
Sometimes, she even went off on treks with her paranormal
club looking for ghosts or other manifestations of the supra-
natural.

"Actually," she said, "the opportunity came up for me to
ask your mother a little about their decision to move to
Miami while I was in Cleveland this past weekend attending
the Golden Seniors Luncheon with her. We were driving
home and she began talking about Florida, about how she
loved it there, how they happened to move there, etc. You
want to hear?"

"I'm all ears."

"Well thirty years ago or so, after your father came
home from Palestine, things weren't so good between them.
She felt he'd been disrespectful by his abandoning her,
leaving her in the dark, so to speak, about what he was going
to do while he was away, and giving her no say over when
and whether he was leaving. Then, there was your Dad's
attitude when he returned home from Palestine. She said that
for a long time he was very distant from her and nothing
seemed to matter to him, almost as if he constantly had
something more important than her on his mind.

"'It was almost as if he had gone back to the old country
ideas of how a woman should be treated," she said. As she
put it, 'He just did what he wanted without discussing it with
me or seeking my agreement.'"

'I never knew what it was all about,' she complained.
'This was at a time when Ben was getting sick on and off
again, and Hymie helped with that, but it seemed like
otherwise he was gone more than he was home. Lester was
in college at the time and he would get angry whenever we
asked him to miss school and go out looking for Ben. Life
was getting pretty bad. At first, I thought maybe Hymie was
just getting tired of all the problems with Ben, and wanting
to get away from them for a while. Then, I started thinking,

maybe it was me—maybe he was angry with me about something.'"

"But this was all happening even before Pa went to Palestine, wasn't it," I asked? "In fact, it's even before he knew he was going to join the Haganah and go overseas. Isn't that true?"

"That's true, but that's when she said it all started—before he went overseas. As she put it, 'They began growing apart toward the end of World War Two, and more so after it ended,' and it was in the months toward the end of 1946 that your Dad sits her down and he tells her that he's leaving; that he's going to Europe with some Jewish agency to look for his brother and sisters, and his relatives; and that he doesn't know when he'll be back. He tells her he knows she can run the store without him, and that he just wants to go. He has to go, he says, but he'll write her from Europe to tell her where he is."

"It wasn't until he came home from Palestine that she actually found out he had sailed with the Aliyah Bet, attempting to smuggle refugees into Palestine at great danger to himself. That in itself greatly hurt her because he never let her in on it while it was happening, and he never sought her advice as to whether he should even do it. It was also a great blow to her upon your father's return from Palestine when she learned he'd found evidence her own father was there but never followed up on it to look for him.

"So to bring them closer together again she suggested that they go down to Florida for a visit to where their friends the Weitzman's had moved. She thought it might be a good idea for the two of them to spend a little time together down there, away from the store and the everyday concerns of living up north. Neither of them had ever been to Florida before, and it seemed like it would be a great vacation for them. The Weitzman's had a home in Key West.

"Your father didn't want to go, and she kind of had to drag him there. In those days, other than by train, the only

way they could get to Florida was to drive. Gas rationing
was over. So they went. The trip took almost twenty-two
hours, and it required them to drive through Miami.

"Having never seen a city like Miami, she fell in love
with it. She also said the city reminded your father of
Odessa, back in the Ukraine, which he had always described
as being beautiful. After they came home she talked to him
many times of moving down to Florida when they retired,
but he would just become distant once again and non-
committal, as if he really didn't care. Finally, when he'd
failed to answer her questions about what was bothering him,
she became exasperated, and she threw him out of the house.
Within three days he was back, hat in hand apologizing and
asking if he could return home.

"But what about the gift," I ask? "What did Ma tell you
about Pa's supposed gift of Miami to her?"

"Oh, we really didn't get that far," Sonia says. "But I
assume that moving to Florida was his way of making all of
this up to your mother."

. . .

The nurse came out of the ICU to update us on how Ma
was doing. All of her vital signs were good—pulse was
strong; heartbeat was regular; blood pressure was closing in
on normal, but she was still very groggy from the anesthetic;
and she had a breathing tube in her mouth. She would not
be moved from recovery to a room in the hospital for another
day or two. When she woke up all the way, she could suffer
from confusion, loss of memory, or have trouble keeping
track of time. There would also be pain from her incisions,
though not heart pain. The nurse suggested that we go home
and come back tomorrow when Ma would be in a better
position to recognize that we were present with her.

I knew there was more to tell from talking in the past to

217

friends of mine who'd had heart attacks.

"What is her current ejection fraction," I snapped?

"Sir, I don't have that information." But the question seemed to cause her alarm, perhaps because she had never had a non-physician ask such a technical question. It related to the amount of blood pumped from Ma's heart with each heart-beat. Anything below an ejection fraction of 30 to 35 was not good.

"Can you describe for me how high up in her anterior descending artery the blockage occurred," I continued?

"No I cannot," came the answer. "You'll have to see the doctor for that information."

I turned to Sonia. "It's obvious we're not going to get any really relevant information about Ma tonight," I said.

"Les, take it easy," Sonia cautioned me. "You'll have a heart attack yourself. So what do you suggest we do?"

"We might as well either check into a motel or go home and come back tomorrow."

"Let's just stay in Cleveland for the night," said Sonia. "I think that would be better than going home and driving back up here in the morning. Either way, you're not going to get too much sleep. I can see that."

TWENTY-SEVEN

They say that children become men, and men become children. Many generations have grown up, become men, and gone hence."

Sholem Aleichem

We stayed at the motel the Cleveland Clinic had on its grounds next door to the hospital. In the morning, I got up before Sonia; wrote her a note that I was going over to see my mother; and quietly left our room at about 7:00 a.m. The motel had a long passageway leading directly to the hospital, and there was a breakfast bar along the way at which I stopped for coffee and a roll. If she wasn't up when I got to the ICU, I would just quietly sit there as she slept until she awakened. There were other people at the breakfast bar who had also apparently passed the long night at the motel, as I had, worried about their loved ones, people, not only from Ohio, but from all over the United States.

"Don't worry," one of them said upon hearing of my mother's plight. "This place is the finest in the world for heart problems. I think the operation your mother had was invented somewhere in New York, but they have greatly perfected it here at the Cleveland Clinic. Why, Saudi kings have even come here to have by-pass surgery I believe. How old is your mother?"

"She's 75."

"Well, I bet her surgery has added another ten to fifteen years of life to her."

Ma was up but very groggy when I finally made it to the ICU. They were just about to remove her breathing tube.

She had passed the night uncomfortably, and now they were giving her something for her pain.

"She's not having pain from the heart," the nurse explained. "Her pain is from her incisions, especially the one they made in her leg to recover the saphenous vein they used for the bypass in her heart. The good news is we'll be moving her from the ICU to a hospital room this afternoon. The bad news is, we're going to keep her for observation longer than originally expected."

"Why is that," I asked?

She avoided the question, encouraging me to ask the doctor instead of her.

I went back to the lounge to wait. Sonia joined me, as did Ben. He was more communicative this morning than he'd been the day before, willing to to talk about the subject of the argument he and Ma had been having just before her heart attack. It was about his second wife.

Shockingly, he said he wanted to leave her. Ma, knowing how difficult he could be at times was, of course, totally against the idea. She didn't want him to be alone, and she probably also wanted someone else to help take care of him if he got sick again.

The argument started while he was explaining his reasons to Ma for wanting to divorce. His first wife, the mother of his children, had been an educated, intelligent, down to earth school teacher, respected in her profession, with the kind of common sense Ben needed to anchor himself. When she died, some thought it was because of the pressure Ben's impractical nature and ethereal personality. She was very stalwart, always seeing him through his bouts of illness, and she was very protective.

His second wife was totally different. She was a woman who enjoyed the party atmosphere of society benefit functions, and she was particularly active in the Cleveland Symphony's fund raising entity, Friends of the Cleveland Orchestra, which each year put on a Gala Evening – Benefit

Concert and Dinner. Ben didn't like her doing this sort of charity work.

As a retiree of the symphony, he had no interest in participating in these various charitable events. So, when he refused to attend, she enlisted the accompaniment of a widower who was on the Symphony Board to stand in for him as an escort. Ben didn't like that. There were many such events, both for the symphony and for other organizations, and Ben would often find himself home alone while his wife was, for all intents and purposes, out with another man for the evening.

Ma had tried to explain to him that he had the choice of either going with his wife to these things, or consenting to allowing another person to stand in for him, and that she was certain if he chose the latter, it would only be on a strictly platonic basis. "I'm sure it's just platonic," she argued. But this did not appease Ben.

"You are a man. Ben, and yet you are still acting like a boy," she told him.

Ben flashed his anger at Ma, disrespectfully telling her that he was tired of her advising him on his relationships with women. The discussion developed into an argument when he, having just lately learned from me of Pa's trip to Palestine, sarcastically quipped that he supposed it would have been alright in Ma's mind, when Pa was overseas, for him to have taken up with another woman, *'strictly on a platonic basis,'* of course.

"You think you know everything," he told her. "But you don't. You really don't know what you're talking about, just as you didn't when you broke Cousin Katie and me up. Platonic relationships often lead to non-platonic relationships."

"For some reason, unknown to me, that comment really set Ma off," he said. "She started yelling at me and then she got sick and I had to call 911. It was all pretty ugly. It brought up memories for her of how she fought to deprive

221

me of my relationship with Cousin Katie and everything else that happened in those dark days." He began tearing up.

I dropped the subject with him immediately. There was no way I wanted to travel back to the disturbing days of the incestuous fog Ma had sought to prevent from gathering around our family by barring the relationship of Ben and Katie.

Ben thought it was Ma's memories of those times that had caused her anger with him, but I wondered if it wasn't something else—namely his hypothetical reference to Pa's having taken up with another woman while overseas. *Had Pa admitted to her that he'd had a relationship with Leila,* I wondered?

. . .

After they moved Ma upstairs into a hospital room, they said we could go in, one at a time, to visit her. I was the first to see her. Her color was good, but she was still very disoriented, confused an groggy. I wondered what they had given her for her pain.

"Where's Hymie," she asked?

"Ma, you know Pa can't be here. He passed away over six months ago. It's me, Lester, your son. I'm here.

A thin smile creased her lips as she struggled to look at me. "Oh, Lazer," she said. "Thank you for coming." Then she was silent as her eyes moved around taking in the room as if for the first time. "But where's Hymie?"

"He died Ma. Think! Remember? Pa died."

"Just like him to leave me when I need him. You know he abandoned me once before when he went to Israel, that's what they call it now--Israel, not Palestine. But I forgave him. That's where he is now, you know, in Israel."

"Did you forgive him Ma?"

"Forgive? Yes. Forget? No."

I don't know what possessed me, but with Ma in this bleary condition, I sensed an opening to learn a little more about what actually happened between her and my father during the period after he returned from Palestine. The question of why Pa wasn't buried in Cleveland still burned inside me. So I overstepped my mission in visiting her. I began asking about Pa.

"So tell me Ma, why did you have Pa buried in Israel?"

That question met with a long silence, during which she closed her eyes, almost as if she was trying to remember. Then she opened them, and she mumbled something I didn't understand.

'Tzadik,' I think she said. After that the silence returned.

"Ma," You don't have to talk about it," I said. It's just that when you said Pa's in Israel right just now, I thought of the fact that he's buried there and I still don't know why he's buried there, or where his grave is in Israel. Where is it?"

"Gilead," she said with forced speech!

"What?"

"Gilead!" She forced the word out of her mouth again!

"Ma. What is Gilead?"

She looked like she was going to fall asleep, so I changed the subject. "How are you feeling? How was your night?"

"*Haleila shlie?* It hurts."

"Where does it hurt?"

"My heart hurts?"

"That's not your heart that's hurting I don't think, Ma," I corrected. "It's your incisions. You're alright. They say you're going to be alright. You had a heart attack and they had to operate on you. They had to open up your chest and break your chest-bone to reach your heart, and then they fixed things up in there. It's called coronary by-pass surgery. The pain you're feeling is because your sternum is now wired back together. It will heal and so will your

223

incisions."

"I don't think that's why. My leg hurts too," she slurred.

"Your leg hurts because they took a vein out of it and put it into your heart to stop the heart attack."

"Heart attack. So that's why my heart hurts."

"No Ma. Try to remember what I said. It's not your heart that's hurting now. Can you remember what was happening before they brought you to the hospital?

"No. Ben's heart was hurting then. Did Ben have a heart attack too?"

"No Ma. Just you. You had a heart attack and Ben called 911."

"No. It was Hymies's heart that was hurting."

"I don't understand Ma. I don't understand what you're saying."

"Ben's heart was hurting. So was Hymie's before Ben's," she mumbled.

I could see she was getting disoriented, and that she couldn't grasp anything having to do with time—what happened before—what happened after, just as the nurse said yesterday she might be when she woke up. It was almost as if she was using her confusion to hide from me.

I decided to leave and let the others have a minute with her. I wasn't sure how things would go when she saw Ben, but I knew he'd want to see her. Maybe Ben and Sonia should visit her together I thought. That might stifle any further eruptions of the fight Ben had had with her. The nurse ok-ed their visiting her together, and I went back to the waiting room.

• • •

When I left Ma's room, I came out to find the rabbi waiting to see her. While Sonia and Ben were in with her, I began asking him questions. "What is Gilead, rabbi," I asked? "Or who is Gilead?"

"Gilead? Gilead is a place often discussed in the Old Testament," he answered, "a mountainous region in the northern part of ancient Israel just east of the Jezreel Valley and the Jordan River. Today, it's in Jordan. It is where the ancient tribes of Israel, Dan, Gad and Reuben, and maybe even Manassah, resided. It's also mentioned in the *Hagadah* we use at Passover, because it's where the ancient prophet Elijah comes from. You've heard the song many times— *Eliahu Hanovi; Eliahu Hatishbi; Eliahu, Eliahu; Eliahu HaGiladi.* Why do you ask?"

"Because my mother's in there talking about it. When I asked her where Pa was buried, she said 'Gilead' twice."

"Oh, oh, oh.! Well it's also roughly the place where your father is buried I believe—Kfar Giladi, which is a kibbutz in northern Israel bearing that name--Gilead. *Giladi* is Hebrew for Gilead. That's where he's buried. Kfar Giladi. It's in Israel, but not far from the place in Trans-Jordan referred to as Gilead in the Bible."

"How did he come to be buried there?"

"Your mother requested it. In fact, she insisted on it. You'll have to ask her why? All I know is that your father fought in a battle there, at some point in time, which she knew about."

"But what did she tell you about Kfar Giladi?"

"Really nothing more than that."

"Did she tell you who his friends were at kibbutz Kfar Giladi, how he happened to be there, where he stayed when he was there?

"No, nothing like that. She simply said that from time to time your father wrote some people there. I believe there was a man named Eitan something or other. I can't remember his last name, and another one named Dani. They are the ones who helped arrange for his body to be picked up at Ben Gurion Airport and buried at Kfar Giladi. It's near an Israeli town called Metula."

225

"Oh, and rabbi tell me this. What is *tzadik?*"

"*Tzadik? Tzadik* is a letter in the Hebrew alphabet. Why do you ask about that?"

"I don't know. Ma mentioned it when I brought up my father while I was in the room with her."

"A *Tzadik* is also a righteous man," the rabbi continued. "In the Talmud it's a title given to righteous Biblical figures, such as prophets, and in Medieval times great spiritual leaders in Judaism were also called *Tzadikim.* It's also the root of the Hebrew words for justice and for charity. I believe your mother thinks of your father as a Tzadik. At least that's what she told me."

"And I have one more question for you, rabbi. What is *Haleila Shlie?*"

"In Hebrew *leila* means 'night.' *Haleila*—'the night'— like in the Four Questions of the *Seder.* You know—*Ma Nishtana haleila hazeh?* 'Why is this night different from all others?' *Haleila shlie* means 'my night', or literally, 'the night is to me.'"

It was clear that Ma had Pa on her mind when I was in her room. But how befuddled was she really? Although confused and disoriented, it appeared she was, in fact, following my questions. And, she was trying to answer them. When I asked her where in Israel Pa was buried, she blurted out the word "Gilead." Now the rabbi was telling me giladi meant Gilead in Hebrew. Had Ma decided to have Pa buried at Kfar Giladi, where he had fought, which was also where the righteous prophet Elijah was from.

Why else would she have requested that he be buried there? When I asked her this, she mumbled Tzadik. Did she consider him to be a Tzadik—a righteous person--like the prophet Elija, who the rabbi said was from Gilead? Even if this was true, that did not seem a very good reason for sending his body all the way to Israel for burial.

Haleila schlei. Haleila schlei? Ma had said "Ha leila schlei It hurts," when I asked her how her night was. The rabbi explained that *schlei* means "my" or "to me," and *leila* is the Hebrew word for night. But *haleila schlei* also contains the name "Leila."--Leila to me hurts? Was that what she dreamed in the night?

TWENTY-EIGHT

"Anger dwells only in the bosom of fools."
Albert Einstein

When Sonia came back from Ma's room, it was all I could do to keep from cross-examining her, but I held off until we were in the car on our way home. I also made a decision. Embarrassing as it might be, I was going to tell her about Leila. I was going to admit I knew my father had a love affair while he was in Palestine with Leila, and that I was concerned that Ma somehow knew about it and was being affected by it.

"How was your visit with Ma," I asked Sonia when we were in the car.

"She's very tired, and she didn't look very good to me. I hope your brother will leave and let her rest soon. I think she needs it."

"Did she seem disoriented while you were with her?"

"No, not really. Just very tired. In fact, she seemed exhausted. Why? Did she seem confused to you?"

"Yes, but actually no. I think her responsiveness to me was the best she could do."

"Wow, well what do you mean by that?"

"Sonia, I have to tell you something. When I was out at Herschel Bloom's farm, I found out that my father had a love affair with a woman named Leila while he was in Palestine, and I'm afraid my mother found out about it. I . . ."

"Wait a minute Les. What are you saying? Your father had an affair in Israel years ago, and we're just now finding out about it?"

". . . That's what I'm saying and more. Ma knows

228

about it."

"And your mother has known about it all these years?"

"Yes."

"How did Bloom know about it?

"My father told him of it."

"Hmm! Hearsay! Sounds like two old men telling each other exaggerated war stories. I wouldn't believe it if I were you."

"No, no, Sonia. If you had heard Bloom tell the story, and all about how my father acted after the affair, you'd believe it. He wasn't bragging about it. He was ashamed of himself, and he wanted to leave Palestine as soon as possible. He was badly conflicted."

Well even if it was true, how would your mother ever have found out about it? From Bloom? I doubt that. From the woman? I doubt that too."

"No. The woman is deceased. She died before my father left Palestine. No I think my father admitted he had an affair to my mother."

"Why would he do that?"

"Because he was ashamed. Because he felt it was the right thing to do. Don't you see? It all makes sense, perfect sense, when you think about it. They were having their problems before he went away to Palestine. Many couples experience problems after 25 years together. Then he ups and leaves her without giving her any details as to where he's going, how he's getting there, or what he's going to do when he gets there. She feels abandoned, and in fact it's almost like she was. His letters are few, far between and not very informational. Then he comes home and tells her everything he's done with the refugees and so forth, and the excitement of it all; and he tells her about evidence of her father being in Palestine—maybe—although he didn't look for her father while he was there.

"She feels completely left out and ignored when she hears all this, especially since Yetta Bloom seems to know

229

much more about what Herschel and your father were doing than she does. She also can't understand why he didn't search for her father if there was evidence he was in Palestine.

"And, when he's finally home with her again, he's distant and not himself anymore, probably because he's still thinking of this woman, Leila, maybe even mourning for her. Finally, not knowing what's wrong, my mother can't take it anymore, and she throws him out. He realizes that now he's truly ashamed of himself and miserable, and he becomes contrite. He comes back home; admits the affair to her; and asks for her forgiveness. She takes him back, and he vows to start over again with her, so he gives her a present, "a present" that she wants very much—retirement in Florida. She has forgiven him because she loves him, and she wants to think of him as a Tzadik, but she has not forgotten, and she cannot forget. Even to this day, she can't talk about it.

"You really believe all this Lester?

"Yes, yes, I think I do."

"Even though you have no real proof your father had an affair, only hearsay? Even though you don't really know if your mother knows about it or not? You really think a man like your father would have the guts to admit this to his wife? Everything you're saying is circumstantial." There's no direct proof."

"Yes, I really believe it all happened that way."

"Well," I don't understand how a traditional person like your mother could cope with such a modern thing as her spouse having an affair outside the marriage."

"That's simple. She pretends it never happened. That's how she copes."

"Well, I just can't believe it. In the absence of direct proof, I just can't believe this happened between your father and your mother as you describe it."

"Well when did you become such a lawyer? What am I supposed to do to get the type of proof you're asking for?

Ask my mother?"

Sonia looked at me and smiled. "Yes, if you've got the guts to ask. It sounds to me like that may be your only way. If you really want to know, that is, although I don't see why you need to know. You willing to risk it?"

"I'm willing to keep talking around it to her and to see if she brings it up. For instance, I'm willing to ask her why she said the word Tzadik today when I was talking to her. I'm also willing to press her a little on why she had Pa buried on a kibbutz named Kfar Giladi near a town named Metula in Israel."

"What is Tzadik?"

"It's a letter in the Hebrew alphabet. I don't want to explain it all now."

"Where's Kfar—whatever, and how do you know that's where he's buried?"

"The rabbi told me."

. . .

Finally, we reach home. It had been a tough three days and I'm exhausted. Sonia is right about one thing for sure. There really is no reason why I need to know if my theory is right, that Pa admitted having an affair with Leila to my mother, and that she had forgiven him. It is still chewing at me, but there is no real necessity for me to know.

As I get into bed, however, I'm still wondering why she had chosen to bury him at Kfar Giladi in Israel? Oh well. After the past three days, I just can't afford another sleepless night to think about it.

Instead, I descend into sleep dreaming about it. I have visions of the attack at Kfar Giladi, and that I am there. I dream that I am there and that Pa is protecting me. I dream that even though Ma has forgiven him, she has decided he didn't deserve to be buried in the same place as her, so she sent his body away to Israel for burial. Then I dream she'd decided, in spite of it all, that Pa was a Tzadik who should be buried in Israel. I dream that she really didn't know about Leila. I even dream that Pa had asked her to have him buried in Israel. At 4:25 a.m. I am awakened by the phone. It's Ben.

"What is it? My god, it's still the middle of the night," I say, clearing my mind of sleep. His voice is grave.

"Les,?" He says "Ma passed away at about 4:07 this morning."

EPILOGUE

This story is an obituary. It's also a tale that crosses two centuries, the fall of a dynasty, two oceans, three major wars, a holocaust, and the birth of a nation. It has been repeated in four languages, one now dead, and another resuscitated after 2000 years, yet all spoken by the same individual. It testifies to the fact that the simplest among us can be persons of valor. It also testifies to the fact that in the end we all come from the same place and we're all going to the same place. The sole measure of a life is what happens in between. That's all that really counts, not monuments, not estates, not buildings or charities named after the deceased, not even what historians write.

Obituary writers fail their subjects and their readers if they write short notices containing mundane content about octogenarians. As of 2018 a person over eighty has lived over one third as long as the United States has existed. In spans of eight decades, transportation has changed from the horse and wagon to the steam engine, and then from steam engines to spaceships. The darkness has been chased away first by candles, then by gaslights, and after gaslights, electric lightbulbs, and then by huge telescopic refractors, while viewing the inner darkness of our bodies has evolved from x-rays, to electrocardiograms to CT scanners. Entire political systems have been born and died. Methods of communication have evolved from flags to radio waves, and from the telegraph to the telephone, to the cell phone, and then to email. Major religions have been invented.

Over a period of eighty years, the American Civil War was endured, two world wars were fought, the War in Viet Nam commenced, and forty-two new countries were

233

recognized by the UN. Curing infections has changed from amputation to the use of anti-biotics, and science has completely eradicated smallpox and almost completely eradicated polio. In the past eighty years we've learned how to delay and stop heart attacks and to replace hearts with heart transplants.

Even the least notable among us cannot have lived longer than eighty years without having done something important, experienced something amazing or participated in something out of the ordinary. Yet only the luckiest of us have, and are, truly loved. Chaim and Anne had that good fortune. They also kept their old traditions and passed into modernity without losing themselves in the process.